THE TWELVE HATS

OF A COMPANY PRESIDENT

What It Takes to Run a Company

by Willard F. Rockwell, Jr.

North American Rockwell Corporation

PRENTICE-HALL, INC.

Englewood Cliffs, N.J.

PRENTICE-HALL INTERNATIONAL, INC., *London*
PRENTICE-HALL OF AUSTRALIA, PTY, LTD., *Sydney*
PRENTICE-HALL OF CANADA, LTD., *Toronto*
PRENTICE-HALL OF INDIA PRIVATE LTD., *New Delhi*
PRENTICE-HALL OF JAPAN, INC., *Tokyo*

© 1971, BY

WILLARD F. ROCKWELL, JR.

LIBRARY OF CONGRESS
CATALOG CARD NUMBER: 77–128084

PRINTED IN THE UNITED STATES OF AMERICA
ISBN-0-13-934166-8
B & P

Foreword

This book talks to me and that is the finest compliment I can pay it. Several times I almost talked back with comments or questions such as "How right!" or "What a good way to put it!" or "Does that approach always work?" or "Do you have any idea how I could apply that ploy to my organization?"

Mr. Rockwell's thoughts fascinated me in two ways. First, as Editor of *Harvard Business Review,* which is published for people such as himself (chairmen, presidents, and presidents-to-be), I find it very necessary to have a clear understanding of how my "customers" think. The author's book is a mirror of the executive mind in action.

Second, as head of my publishing operation, I face many of the same situations that chief executives confront. Not on the same scale, of course. But with an international circulation of well over 100,000, and with the complex inter-relationships among editorial, subscription promotion and fulfillment, advertising sales, and production—*and* the people to man those functions—the hats I have to wear are no fewer than twelve.

The significance is clear: this book is going to be of value. Not just to heads of large corporations, but also to those dynamic executives who run smaller businesses on the grow. And the value —as it has been to me—will be in sharing Al Rockwell's ideas, such as the many concrete suggestions gleaned from his rich experience and wide observation. Or, perhaps even more, in sharing the spirit with which he tackles problems and opportunities. The author has made that live.

The entire business community will warmly applaud this book!

Ed Bursk
Editor
Harvard Business Review

Changing Hats
in the Biggest Game of All

Where do corporation presidents come from? Every study seems to come up with a different answer. One survey indicated that men with financial skills have been taking over an ever-larger number of executive suites in recent years, but that the trend appears to be leveling off. Another study showed that the Ivy League has lost ground to the Big 10 as a maker of presidents, and that very few went to private prep schools and even fewer are in the Social Register. Still another study revealed that Utah supplied the highest percentage of company presidents in relation to population of any state in the union.

The fact is that a president can come from just about anywhere—any state, any school, any specialty, and, as the age-old barriers come tumbling down, any neighborhood or national background. I assume that a great many young men and probably quite a few young women in this country of ours are aspiring to head up a great corporation. It is an admirable goal. And yet I often wonder if many of them know what the job is really all about.

What, after all, does a president *do*? I'm reminded of a piece I read somewhere about a theatrical director who, it seems, was having great difficulty in explaining *his* job to the members of a civic group. In the question-and-answer period after his talk, one interested lady rose to inquire just what the director actually did in putting on a play. At some length, the speaker went into details about interpreting the author's intentions, coordinating elements such as scenery, lighting and costumes, and his psychological coaching of the actors.

The light dawned. "Oh, I see," the woman said. "You're the one who tells the actors when to come on the stage and when to go off."

He sighed and gave up. "And when to sit down. Yes, that's it."

It wasn't the woman's fault that she could only understand the superficial parts of the job. What a stage director actually does is complex, subtle, hard to get at. And it's the same with a president or chief executive officer of a company. At first glance, I suppose, the president is the one who "tells everybody in the company what to do." In fact, of course, he does no such thing. The job is even more difficult to pin down than that of the theatrical director.

Perhaps a company president tells his "actors" how to come and go, but he also involves himself in a fantastic amount of professional enterprise. He deals with just about every discipline known to man, with many of which he himself has only a passing acquaintance.

It is by far the most fascinating job I know. I've bagged rabbits with a .22 and I've hunted elephants. But the biggest game I know is business. *That's* where you get the fast results of decisions, the endless opportunity to test yourself, the daily chance to contribute something good out of your own abilities.

There are more chances to contribute today than ever before. We're constantly challenged by our changing environment—water, air and land. New concepts of urban living are changing the face of America. Advancing technology keeps opening doors to invention. Automation is forcing all of us toward higher personal development.

American business and industry are at the center of all these challenges, with a thousand contests going on at once—all of which need people who want to contribute in a hurry.

Not long ago there was a day when I shifted "roles" three or four times in a matter of hours. One moment I was *judging* the abilities of a potential new division head; next I was *exploring* new processing techniques with our research and development chief; later I was *selling* the owner of a small company on joining forces with us. Late that afternoon a close associate who'd been with me all day said: "Al, you wear more hats than Red Skelton."

The thought intrigued me. So I did, at that. One night I counted up my "hats"—or separate but related functions as head of a company—and came up with a total of, ironically enough, exactly 12: Skipper, Pioneer, Soothsayer, Impresario, Marathon Runner, Lord Chief Justice, Student, Reporter, Coach of Champions, Crusader, Miner, Super-salesman. I show in this book why these hats must be a part of every president's wardrobe if he is to accurately gauge the winds of change and set his sails on course.

These hats represent roles. Each covers a multitude of psychological nuances, off-beat techniques and little known strategies of successful executive leadership. No hat is for the timid, because business is no pink tea party. They are to be used. Sometimes one will be enough to "bring home the coonskin." Sometimes two, three or four must be worn. Many's the day when I have worn all twelve hats at once! The big trick is to juggle the twelve hats, and I show you how in this book.

Do you have to be a president to benefit from this book? Not at all. This book is for every dynamic businessman with his eye on the helm.

If you make maximum use of the Twelve Hats of a President you will be putting into action proven strategies for making green the profit fields of your company. And that's what separates presidents from ordinary men.

WILLARD F. ROCKWELL, JR.

Contents

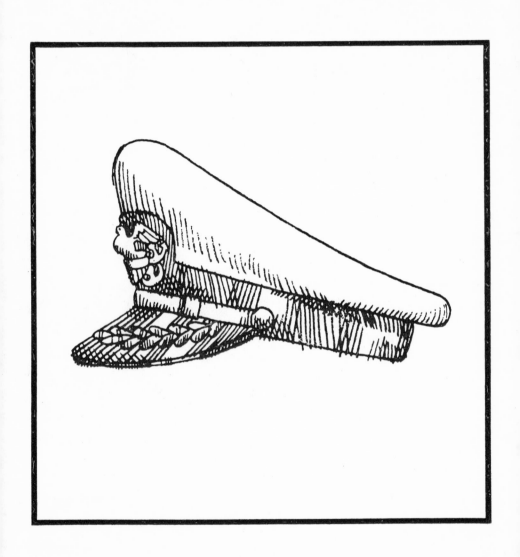

CHAPTER ONE

The Hat of the Skipper

In Japan, where the average businessman stays with the same company all his life and where hardly anyone ever gets fired, they have an interesting way of making decisions. The management group gets together and talks it over at great length. And after quite a long time, a decision emerges out of that group. No one individual gets the credit—or the blame.

Now don't get me wrong. I am not scorning the Japanese way of managing business enterprises. They have much to teach us, particularly when it comes to *implementing* decisions. Once the group *does* make up its collective mind, the Japanese can move with astonishing speed. Just ask anyone who has ever tried to match wits with them in exports!

Nor am I going to criticize the methods of the Europeans, many of whom also tend to favor committee rule. But I will say that the traditional American concept of individual responsibility has a lot going for it.

We feel that the head of a company must take complete responsibility for its progress and safety—not unlike the responsibility of the captain of a ship at sea. And below the president, each individual manager is also skipper of his own craft, his own unit of the fleet. The concept works for us.

And it has had a great deal to do with the much-discussed explosion of American industrial might all over the world. When they warn their countrymen about the dangers of U.S. industrial domination, foreigners like Jean-Jacques Servan-Schreiber call attention to our organizational abilities first of all. It's not just our resources and our cash; it's also our system, our methods that make us so powerful, they say. And surely the first principle of the American business system is this idea of giving the man at the top total and complete responsibility for what happens to his company. He is the skipper, and if the ship runs into an iceberg, it's his fault.

"We may double earnings next year," the president of one of the newer conglomerates told me over dinner, "or we may slip back. If we do, our stock will fall right out of bed and the stockholders will have my neck. And rightly so. Although I get a tremendous amount of good help and advice, the decisions in the last analysis are mine."

I am aware that there are management experts who see a gradual trend in U.S. business toward participative decisions, a kind of consensus management. But I think they mistake manner for method. What *is* changing, and changing fast, is the *way* the executive makes his decision. In the old days, he used to take counsel mainly with the Almighty, then make a decision based on intuition. These great intuitive managers built not only their companies, but also American industry as we know it, and we owe them much. Proper use of intuition is still a great asset. But nowadays we are also scientific. We avail ourselves of all sorts of specialized expertise. We get the participation of our subordinates right down the line. But finally we—meaning the top executives of corporations—must assume the burden for each and every major decision.

A climate of risk-taking must exist in every successful company. No one in the company will take the necessary chances unless he knows that his chief is unafraid.

Let me go further: No one in the company will do much of anything that is effective unless he has full confidence in the ultimate boss. The institution must be, as Emerson said, "the lengthened shadow of one man"—even as huge and complex an institution as a great corporation.

You, the chief executive, must carry your company. Like that greatest of all weightlifters, Atlas, you must take this particular world on your shoulders.

Otherwise . . . well, let's see what has actually happened when presidents failed to carry the burden:

THE CASE OF THE MUDDLED MERGER

This is a classic story of merger mismanagement. Acquisition specialists never tire of talking about the leading consumer products company that missed a chance to acquire Royal Crown Cola several years ago. The company's top managers evidently didn't turn their personal attention to the merger, but turned it over to a staff group. This group studied what it knew best—Royal Crown's financial structure—and decided that R.C. wasn't a good buy.

Two months later, R.C. launched its Diet-Rite Cola, which quickly became the front runner in the low-calorie soft drink market. What should have been studied, then, was not the financial structure but the marketing plans of Royal Crown. But the staff group missed that angle entirely because top management hadn't given it the proper direction.

THE CASE OF THE ABSENTEE LANDLORD

This time it was the other side that goofed. This small New England manufacturer was ready to sell out. The word got around and soon a large midwestern company opened serious negotiations. The smaller firm had a good reputation and sound structure, and it seemed to fit into the pattern of acquisitions the midwesterners had been following. Everything looked good—except for one problem.

The midwestern company had no one available to take over management of the firm, and had no intention of scouting around for a divisional president. The New England company's current management would have to continue in charge. And where was the president who wanted to sell out, while these negotiations were going on? He had gone fishing. Aboard his yacht, in the Caribbean. He was an able man, but as the inheritor of a small private company that had been in his family for generations, he was conspicuously lacking in drive and determination.

The midwesterners decided that, yachtsman though he was, they couldn't trust him to skipper the company ship. So they turned the acquisition down. Later the playboy president had to settle for a far less attractive deal with another firm.

THE CASE OF THE FEUDING BARONS

Decentralization is a policy that has spread into many areas of U.S. industry. It can work, but it can also get out of hand. The problems come when the various divisions engage in what British consultant Antony Jay calls "baronial warfare." This was the case with General Dynamics in the early 1960's. The new president found that he lacked effective authority over the company's nine large and powerful divisions.

Says Jay in his admirable book, *Management and Machiavelli*, "As a result of its feudal, baronial structure, General Dynamics managed to lose $425 million between 1960 and 1962, the biggest product loss ever sustained by any company anywhere."

THE CASE OF THE IVORY TOWER

This is the short, tragic story of an electronics genius who didn't know his own limitations. Basically an inventor, he took his patents and started a small but highly sophisticated business. As it began to grow, he realized he needed a practical mind in top management to run the show. So he brought in a competent general manager—but failed to give him full authority.

For every important move, the general manager had to come in and get permission from the owner, who was usually tinkering happily in the laboratory. Needless to say, the company went through a series of general managers. Finally the owner realized that he himself was the main obstacle to the company's efficient operation. So he hired still another g.m. and gave him absolute authority. He himself just stayed in the lab.

That didn't work, either. In the middle of a delicate expansion program involving large capital expenditures, the general manager suddenly died. Naturally there was no trace of backup management. The owner had no idea what was going on. His company sustained a multimillion dollar loss, the first of several setbacks that led to its being placed in receivership.

THE CASE OF THE ETERNAL COMMITTEE

A few years go a New York consulting firm came up with a mathematical formula for one of top management's most common problems—the acceptance or rejection of proposals from the research and development department. Will the idea cost millions and be a flop—or will it cost millions in lost business if you do not try it? The consultants had a formula that they said was as simple "as a child's textbook."

Did the formula actually work? I have no idea. I don't know of any company that ever seriously tried it.

But I do know of several that obtained the formula—and then spent a considerable amount of money having it evaluated by *other* consulting firms.

As an observer said at the time: "Will *somebody* please make a decision?"

We needn't belabor the point. In all these cases the top manager of a company simply abdicated his responsibility, with disastrous results. He had something else to think about which he believed to be more important. Or he delegated himself into a hole. Or he didn't have the ability in the first place.

WHAT GOES ON IN THE CAPTAIN'S LOG

Now let's be a little more specific. Every president, as I've said, must carry the weight of the company on his shoulders. That means, first of all, setting the basic course which the company will follow. There are a number of things that a president must simply make up his mind about, with no vacillating, before he can even begin to direct operations.

Here are a few of these basic decision areas:

1. How can you keep up with market changes—or initiate them?

Nothing is more crucial today. One of the mournful roll calls of industrial history is the list of companies that continued to make widgets and whatsits long after the world had lost interest in widgets and whatsits. The list of companies that followed or led the market, on the other hand, includes all the great success stories of U.S. and foreign enterprise. And more are coming along all the time, from small electronics companies that see a coming need for some tiny component that they have developed, to the huge tobacco companies that are fighting a rearguard action in their prime industry while using their capital to move aggressively into more secure fields in other products.

Computers, of course, have proved a great aid in short-term

forecasts of marketing results, especially in the more predictable industries that are subject to easily recognized indicators. A company like American-Standard, for instance, can use "exponential smoothing" to put its entire sales forecast process on the computer as a check against the manual process. But this works only if housing continues to use traditional plumbing and heating equipment. No computer and no programmer can predict a technical breakthrough that might throw all calculations out the window. Presidents do that—with the help of everyone in their companies.

At North American Rockwell we have set up a fairly elaborate "Business Opportunities Identification and Development System." The flow chart that goes with it shows how an idea for a new product or application goes through a series of checks and reviews on the way to "Decision to Pursue," and then further to "Launch Project." Various managers and committees (including a Technology Exploitation Committee) are brought into the process at specific points. There are several places where the idea may fall into a box marked "Hold for later consideration" or "Discard" (file).

But what I want to emphasize here is that the whole system starts in the marketplace rather than the lab. The first box represents a "Surveillance System" through which many people in the company identify possible market needs.

This doesn't mean that we never get a new product idea out of research without first considering the market need. It only means that at every opportunity we try to turn our thinking around so that we proceed from market need to product, instead of the often disastrous reverse. We call the process "Marketback."

That's our way of trying to keep our company from becoming, at some future date, obsolete.

2. How should you direct research activities?

It's an old, old headache. If you tell your research people to concentrate on practical solutions to anticipated problems, they may not come up with the basic discovery that might revolutionize an industry and make your company another Xerox. On the other hand, if you let them concentrate on basic research you may not only get no return from the research investment for an indefinite period of time, but you may also actually fall behind in current developments in your line.

There's no simple answer to this, as we know at North American Rockwell after a few years of dedicated and increasingly successful attempts to apply exotic space research to the commercial marketplace. Most companies would like their Research and Development to include both basic and applied science. But for companies not large enough for this, there are ways of getting access to the kind of research that is lacking.

There are technology development companies that can take your idea and make something useful out of it, either on straight assignment or as a joint venture. We have used them ourselves in areas where we lacked expertise. And, of course, a wise chief executive never stops searching the printed pages, the conversation of acquaintances, and even the countryside to find new ideas that might prove useful to his company.

Many times, of course, inventors will come to you with what they consider important breakthroughs. At least 90 percent of these will not prove out, but you must take the time to have these ideas checked out anyway. You can't afford to cut yourself off from the wellsprings of creativity.

As for basic research, my belief is that even this can profit from some direction from topside. Contrary to the popular view, scientists are not always divorced from commercial reality. You can help by keeping in close communication with research people. Bring scientists into your higher councils. When someone originates a promising idea, have your research director bring him to the management meeting to explain it. There is no substitute for this eyeball-to-eyeball contact.

Incidentally, the same applies to market research. As the marketing director of Kollsman Instrument Corporation once remarked: "Some of the things that market researchers most like to do— things that really get them excited—turn out to be the least useful to management." He was talking about broad studies of the company's market position on a particular product, how it breaks down by geography and so on.

The best market research, this executive said, should have a sales direction. For instance, several years ago Kollsman told its marketing research people to find out why it wasn't having any luck selling its aeronautic instruments to business jet manufacturers even though it was predominant in the large commercial jet market. The researchers found that the business jets were using rebuilt instruments of Korean War vintage that cost as little as one-fifth the price of the new instruments, yet worked perfectly.

Kollsman thus knew it would be wasting its time trying to crack that market at the time. And then the market researchers went further and made a projection of when this surplus instrument market would dry up—signalling the time when Kollsman should make a concentrated effort to get the newly available business.

All this worked beautifully—because market research had been given direction from the highest levels of the company.

3. What organizational guidelines should you use?

Should you allow decentralization to undermine home office authority? On the other hand, should you allow centralization to undermine divisional initiative and responsibility? Another of those age-old problems. Don't expect me to solve it for you. It's up to you, after careful analysis of your company's special conditions and situations, to make up your mind about this.

Organizational problems have a way of drifting. If you don't take hold, your company will just slip into decentralization without your even knowing what's happening. That may or may not be good. In the same way, the total size of the company might get completely out of hand. Nowadays management experts talk about the "critical mass," which is the supposed ideal size and makeup for a given company. But it's all too easy to ,let the departments reproduce themselves—their reasons for adding personnel are always so convincing!—until you have layers of fat at every level of management and supervision.

"If a company has 'executivitis' at the top, the disease will eventually spread to all of the tentacles of the business," says consultant James J. Hickey. I can think of at least one large company, a famous name in American industry, that is a perfect example of this "executivitis." It just keeps on adding new departments and new managers and new staff groups, and reducing its efficiency almost every time. Yet the company is always sending its people to seminars to make learned speeches on how to perform all the major and minor functions of industrial management. Like some ballplayers, they talk a good game. But they move slowly and hesitantly and are being quickly outdistanced in the marketplace by many far smaller and less powerful outfits.

4. How much inter-company rivalry should you allow?

At companies like General Motors, each large division is encouraged to try to outdo the other, with independent marketing programs and other functional groups. This has many good effects for the same reason that free competition between companies has good effects. But there are also problems such as lost opportunities for cooperation.

The same holds true for any company. Should you encourage healthy competition between divisions—and for that matter, between individuals? The old procedure was to put a couple of strong men in a competitive situation and, by letting them slug it out, seeing which one could rake in the most profits for the company. Nowadays there are movements in the other direction. The management task force, cutting across departmental and divisional lines for a joint solution of some common problem, is getting more and more popular.

American Airlines, which stressed competition in its management training not long ago, is now emphasizing cooperation between functions. Instead of management games in which teams would compete against each other for hypothetical profits, American now uses exercise situations in which conflicts are ironed out through "tradeouts." The instructors examine, for instance, the situations in which operations people, with clear instructions to have a plane take off exactly at 3 o'clock, look down the ramp to see a passenger running for the gate at 2:59.

As this is written, cooperation is the big thing in many industries. But where does that leave the individual responsibility we were talking about? As the company's fleet commander, don't you want subordinate skippers in every ship down the line, willing to shoulder their own burdens come what may?

Again, no easy answer. This is just another of the problems you as president will be called on to ponder.

5. How involved should the company be in social problems?

Here's a question that will be increasingly on the minds of company presidents in coming years. Should you participate in such things as government job-training programs? What are your company's responsibilities to community renewal, pollution control, education? How about corporate support of the arts? We're always hearing about our neglect in that sector.

Here's another one: How will you react when called on to provide a plant for some "new city" being built with government funds out on the Great Plains, perhaps, far from existing metropolitan areas? As population pressures increase, calls for projects like this will get more and more insistent.

No matter how you personally feel about the company's social responsibility, how will you sell what you do to your stockholders, one way or the other?

6. What should the main thrust of the company be in the next decade or so?

Is this a time for expansion or consolidation? Should you concentrate energies on the development of new products or on the refinement of existing ones? What are the main problems to be solved? Are they in the realm of distribution, plant modernization, organization, management development, acquisitions, or just what?

And once you decide which are the most critical areas, you have to decide (1) how you will go about attacking these problems, and (2) to be honest, what individual can best solve them after your retirement. At some point in your career you will be giving a great deal of thought to the next skipper for the company. If you have been a success, the board of directors will naturally listen carefully to your recommendations. And this is perhaps the supreme test of the chief executive's powers of reason and detachment. Forget about picking "your kind of guy." You'll have to pick the man you honestly and unemotionally believe can best lead the company through the trials you have forecast. And then you must be sure he's ready to assume the heavy burden when the time comes.

SOME SKIPPERS SINK

Now we come to the crucial point: How do you become a fully qualified captain? How do you develop the psychological strength to take full responsibility?

You may very well already have this strength. If you are any-where close to the top of a company, if you are even a remote candidate for the post of president, you surely have it in you somewhere.

It's true that industry is afflicted by a certain amount of charla-tans. These "corporate parasites," as consultant John L. Handy calls them, get by in fairly responsible jobs by brain-picking their betters and amusing the office crowd with their charming per-sonalities. They can get by for years, probably for an entire career, by "winging it," without tipping off the fact that they have no real knowledge or skills and haven't an idea in their heads. Yes, we have these parasites in business—but very few if any ever get into the top ranks.

If you move toward the summit, chances are you have the po-tential to be a fleet admiral. But will this potential come out? Here are some of the things that might stifle it.

OVER-DEPENDENCE ON EXPERTS

This is one of the greatest obstacles to presidential control. In the technical arena, we have all manner of strange and exotic new products and processes that seem understandable only to NASA scientists. We also have a technological explosion that leads to ever-narrowing disciplines, so that a project that might have called for one Ph.D. five years ago now requires the services of five Ph.D.'s and two psychiatrists.

In computers, as if the vast new forecasting and real time system weren't confusing enough, we have other experts making econometric models to predict return on investment, and other mathematical models to predict changes in an entire economy.

We have linear programming of project planning, decision net-works to help choose between alternative solutions, and of course we have so much emphasis on interpersonal relations that, one consultant tells us, within a few years large companies will have a behavioral scientist as a key member of the management team.

All these new management sciences are simply tools for making wiser and quicker executive decisions. Industry has come to the point where we can hardly do without them. But to be able to make intelligent use of these tools, the president must at some point perform an act of faith. He must accept what his technicians tell him. It has been pointed out—correctly—that an executive doesn't have to know how a computer works in order to make use of the information it supplies to him. Sure, but how do you know your EDP man knows how it works? That's perhaps an oversimplification, but you see what I mean.

The chief executive should continually question his experts, try to trip them up if he can. What happens more often is that presidents become too trusting, too willing to accept what they are told. This can happen even to the president with a technical background, because not only academic degrees but also technical experience becomes obsolescent these days—almost as soon as it is acquired.

But there is still another type of expert on whom a president can become over-dependent. These are the practitioners of what you might call the arts of industry. Public relations, for instance. Or graphic arts. Listen to a public relations man telling you why the annual report should carry a candid photograph of the chairman of the board scratching his nose. Or listen to the graphic artist as he shows slides of the proposed new trademark and outlines how this "solution" will reflect the traditions of the company since 1875 and yet hint somehow that its equipment will soon be used in some moon colony!

This is not to disparage the art of the corporate graphics expert. We recently engaged one (Saul Bass Associates) to design a new trademark for us. And we agree with him that the new mark represents qualities like "vast resources, vitality, uniqueness and pioneering." But dealing in these concepts is not easy for a business executive.

There is no way to prove these men right or wrong, even when you accept their suggestions. As they themselves will tell you, no one can say how much the company "image" contributed to profits. We know from studies that our public awareness increased with the new trademark, but we can't prove it made us any money. Advertising results, on the other hand, are somewhat more demonstrable, but even here there is little certainty of cause-and-effect.

An example

The president of one consumer goods company invested heavily in package design for a new product he was bringing out. A design firm experimented for many weeks and then came up with an elaborate, extremely colorful package that was beautiful to look upon but complicated to use. To the president, the package didn't quite seem to fit in with the nature of the product. His judgment, based not on anything specific but simply on the "feel" of years of experience, was that this package wasn't right.

But the designers changed his mind with their color slides and their scientific sounding "evidence." He okayed the package. The product came out and was a pronounced failure.

"I should have told them to try again, no matter how certain they were," the president admitted after the losses were in. "That's what I'm being paid for."

LACK OF FULL UNDERSTANDING

Businessmen, with their constant concerns and time-consuming administrative chores, are notoriously narrow people, or so it is often said. We are supposed to be uninformed about matters outside our commercial interests, and generally lacking in taste or discrimination or intellectual attainments. The corniest farce of the Broadway season is always described as fare for the "tired businessman."

If there ever was any justice in that description of the businessman, there is very little now. Businessmen now are among the broadest and most concerned of citizens, by and large. Make sure you keep up with this trend—not to amaze your friends with the brilliance of your conversation, especially, but for the more practical reason that you need to be well-rounded to be a good businessman in this age.

Lack of insight and perspective can easily keep a president from exercising that full responsibility. If you feel ignorant about the customs and traditions of the country where you're building a new plant or opening distribution, you might fail to make the necessary decisions. You may become fatally hesitant. Or just as bad, you may close your eyes and blunder through.

Each summer hundreds of executives turn up at campuses like Williams or the University of California or dozens of others to study philosophy, great books, and so on. One John Hancock man who attended a course at Williams a couple of years ago made this comparison:

In business you analyze things to find the best course of action. You make an analysis here, too, but the difference is in the subject matter, which takes you out of the normal realm of thinking and forces you to read just to the importance of these other problems.

In other words, your mind is "expanded" (without benefit of drugs, at that). The executive who has broadened himself in this manner, or who has always been blessed with a wide range of interests, is all the better able to read with confidence. He sees aspects of things and situations that narrower men do not see. Very likely, his outlook is tempered with humor. And he probably has a certain modesty which all the same does not keep him from feeling that he has the ability to command men older, more experienced, better educated, and perhaps richer than himself.

Above all, he takes the long view of his company's place in the scheme of things, and his own—without for a moment failing to concentrate on the vitally important matters of immediate and short-term concern.

If you think I'm saying that a successful company president should also be something of a philosopher—you're right.

FAILURE TO FOLLOW UP

And this, of course, is more than anything else what causes the would-be skipper to go off course. Which outgoing President of the United States was it who said of his successor: "Poor ———. He'll tell people to do this and do that and then he'll wonder why it is that nothing ever gets done." Never mind who it was. No use getting politics into this. The point is that this particular President was sure that the incoming Chief wouldn't know how to work through the bureaucratic mass of Washington to see that his directives actually were carried out.

You can't just *make* decisions. You must also *follow them up.* Commented an executive of W. R. Grace & Co.: "If the executive doesn't live with his decision and see it through to a successful conclusion, it can come back to haunt him."

This means, among other things, that you must make sure that the people who report to you do their own share of skippering, too. You must insist that they produce, and that they are willing to assume burdens. They must be willing, for instance, to argue with you when they feel they are right and you are wrong.

But it also means that you must have some system for making sure that your decisions, when you make them after due deliberation and consultation, are in fact carried out. A concept called "closed loop" control is one idea that has been advanced by Professor Jay W. Forrester of M.I.T. The basic idea is that through regular meetings and periodic reports the chief executive (and every other decision-making executive) gets a continuous relay of signals back to him which not only tell him how the directives are being carried out but also indicate what further action should be incorporated into the whole.

Whatever system you use, remember that no decision means anything until the order is carried out.

THE CAPTAIN'S TABLE

No one is so certain of his skills that he can't stand a little practice. A couple of years ago, for instance, the *New York Times* reported that in a computerized New York University business game, the "directors" of the companies (real executives and professors) were learning as much as the students (NYU graduate students). One board advised its student management not to discuss a certain demand of the union in labor negotiations, because it was a prerogative of management. But the union struck (said the computer) according to NLRB rulings, and the company went from first to last place in its industry because of a two-month strike.

The *Times* added that a couple of the "directors" had been so intrigued that they signed up for the course.

Which is to say that we are all only human. We make our decisions, confident as can be that we are right, yet aware in our secret thoughts that we could be wrong.

The Hat of the Skipper is first on the shelf. It's the basic item in any president's apparel. If you can't stand almost crushing responsibility, none of the other Hats will do much for you.

If, however, you can be Skipper, the prizes are great. In my own case, I live a life that I regard as enviable. There are physical luxuries. More than that, there are intellectual and cultural rewards. A ranking executive has the opportunity to meet and get to know a variety of interesting, exciting people. Not only businessmen, but also statesmen, theatrical people and others—all men and women of substance and achievement. Finally, there is the stimulation of travel, much of it in the company of my wife, Constance.

The travel is not all business, of course. We love sightseeing, swimming, fishing, and antiquing, and we also love to go on safari and do so at every opportunity. I work many, many long hours, and to me most of it is fun, but I also find or make the time for other forms of fun.

I am proud to have been able to provide this kind of existence for my family. Constance enjoys our style of life as much as I, and so do our daughter and four sons. And that, of course, is what makes it all worthwhile, including those headaches that you sometimes get from wearing 12 Hats at the same time.

"Man's capacity for handling information is limited. He has a narrow bandwidth, a high noise level, is expensive, and works intermittently." The quote comes from a lady psychologist, Gene Livingston of IBM, who nevertheless believes that there is a place for man (or woman) in the information-oriented industrial world of the future.

"We can compensate for these human disadvantages by designing systems which make maximum use of man's special talents," Dr. Livingston assures us. "Man should be considered a component in any such design system.

"Man is best suited for translating information, reacting to unexpected low-probability events, and exercising judgment where events cannot be completely defined. There are times when it may not be clear which system element is most appropriate for carrying out a particular task. Whether an erase function is performed by hardware or programming might depend upon usage, cost of a buffer, etc. . . ."

Dr. Livingston was talking about the people who operate and work with the computer, of course—not the president who sits several stories above or below, and tries to make decisions on the basis of what the EDP department and others tell him. But she could have been talking about you—the president, the skipper, the boss of the whole shooting match.

It is you who must be good at "exercising judgment when events cannot be completely defined"—and taking the full responsibility for it.

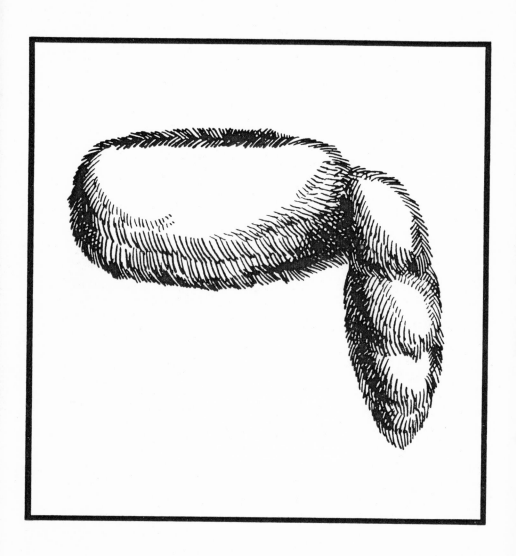

CHAPTER TWO

The Hat of the Pioneer

"Gentlemen, we have two choices before us: to innovate, or to vegetate." A president I know recently made that statement in a Founder's Day speech. It drew applause. But if the president had been truly objective, he might have added: ". . . and we, gentlemen, have chosen the second alternative."

This chief executive was sincere in his sentiment, honest in his intention. His company, however, was and is miles behind the competition in developing new products and new ideas. Top management preaches innovation—but holds new ideas "for further consideration." The company has more committees per square foot than any other outfit in that part of the country. It suffers, in general, from a kind of corporate senility.

And it's not alone. The situation is far from uncommon in companies of all sizes and ages. Some of the small, young companies are just as senile as the stodgiest old-line giant. And the reason, of course, is that the president has left his coonskin cap hanging on the wall.

The Hat of the Pioneer is more than an ornament. In Pittsburgh, which has been my headquarters all my business life, the American pioneer is part of our heritage. Those tall men who crossed the Alleghenies to Fort Pitt, then pushed farther west, wore their fur caps like a badge. Sure, they kept the head warm, which was important. But they also proclaimed in no uncertain terms that here was a man capable of challenging and conquering the wilderness, which in those days meant the vast majority of what is now the United States of America.

As likely as not, the quality of the cap showed how good a marksman the wearer was. A pioneer could shoot his clothing as well as his food.

There must be something of that tough independence, that willingness to "make tracks into the unknown," as Thoreau phrased it, in every corporate president. And it's not enough just to talk about this traditional pioneer spirit. You must truly have it, act upon it, and see that others do the same.

I can cite one company which, 15 years ago, scrambled to the forefront of its industry with a rash of new products and product modifications. But in more recent years this company lost ground to younger-thinking, more dynamic competitors. The company was still riding the waves of past achievement, and the president had sufficient vision to realize this. So he appointed a committee of one consisting of the engineer and scientist who, to a large degree, had been responsible for the successful innovation of a decade and a half before. His sole job from here on out would be to explore new products, new processes, new service ideas, and come up with suggestions for change.

Well intentioned though the move was, it failed. In the end, no really substantial ideas came to light. What the president had not taken into consideration was that the scientist, now six years away from retirement, was a man who had already "made it." He was no longer the up and coming driver and thruster of 15 years ago. He was set in his ways, unwilling to put his neck on the block and take the risk that is the inevitable sidekick of innovation. Here again, as is so often the case, the move towards innovation was little more than lip service on the part of the chief executive.

I think there is much truth to a statement made by Donald A. Schon of Arthur D. Little, Inc. in *Think* magazine. ". . . companies become trapped in a conflict of policy and practice. It is company policy to seek innovation, and company practice . . . to resist it."

Talented managers, of course, are quick to sense this double talk. Inspired by the call to arms, they are soon deflated by the failure to attack. As a result the idea flow is turned off. Or worse, creative comers take their thinking to the competition where they are hopeful of a warmer and more profitable reception.

HOW TO BLAZE THE TRAIL

In my experience, if the chief executive's coonskin cap is frequently and prominently displayed, key subordinates will be quick to take the cue and don innovator hats of their own.

In practice the innovator will be regarded as either a hero or an upstart. It depends on the operating climate. One young manager I know suggested a rather radical marketing proposal to his boss. It was not only turned down, but was also greeted with obvious disapproval. The young man was properly repentant until a competitor introduced a similar program successfully. At that point, the young man quietly packed his bags.

How much innovation is enough? Where is innovation most desirable? How much time should scientists, engineers, managers devote to searching for new ideas? "Give them free rein," some will urge. But that's not always a realistic approach. I know managers who would devote full time to idea exploration if given the chance. It is not easy for men of ideas—or their superiors—to define boundaries. Some managers focus innovational effort in unprofitable areas. Others hold back for fear of being presumptuous. Too many talented people lack the direction and guidance they need.

Pioneering leadership, I think, must come from the president. And his pioneering pose should extend beyond the popular ploy of pop talk participation. As one president puts it:

> If I have the right to expect innovation from my people, they have the right to expect me to lead the way with more than high-sounding words. It's the chief's job to establish the rules of the game. On the one hand, he must see to it that experimentation is encouraged and initiative rewarded. On the other hand, he must properly channel innovation so that it will not go hogwild. The best contribution a president can make is to adopt a constantly challenging attitude in areas of prime concern. In my view, a relentless search for that simpler, better, more imaginative way to do the job can't help but pay off.

I am a great believer in this philosophy. I find that when you send people back again and again in search of more profitable alternatives, in time they acquire this habit of exhaustive probing on their own.

Another aspect of concern to the would-be innovator is this problem of risk. Innovation implies inexperience. It creates a need for knowledge about new methods, new materials, new areas of technology. Where inexperience and the need for training exist, confidence fades, uncertainty creeps in. The degree of risk multiplies. In my observation, the *fear* of failure serves more than any other factor to stifle initiative and keep men welded to the status quo. I think if a president realistically expects his people to venture forth into unknown fields, he must first recognize that an increased likelihood of errors exists. Then he must convince his people that he regards such mistakes as investments in progress, not as a quick route to early retirement.

As one businessman remarked recently: "Mistakes are building blocks, the price you have to pay for improvement. The manager who never makes mistakes lives in a vacuum, and that's the biggest mistake of all."

SET INNOVATIONAL PRIORITIES

In attempting to multiply your company's idea output, where should you start? "Anywhere and everywhere," many will say, and a good argument could be made for this point. No product, no program, no system is so good it cannot be made better. Just the same, I think it is a good idea to set priorities.

Misdirected initiative can be even more costly than passivity. The trick, as we have learned at North American Rockwell, is to pinpoint problem areas where change is clearly called for. Obviously, if performance is sliding, if programs are bogged down, if morale is at a low ebb, you must be doing something wrong and should be doing something new. Accurately identifying problem areas and attacking these with fresh ideas, we have found, maximizes your chance of success. With resistance to change overcome by the need, programs and ideas are easier to sell. On the other hand, where innovation is poorly targeted, it causes bad situations to worsen and structural rigidity to solidify.

One unfortunate chief executive I can call to mind learned this the hard way. For decades his company had been a successful producer of natural products. But some years ago it found itself plagued by market inroads made by bold new manufacturers of the same products fabricated out of synthetic materials. The financial statements showed sales declining, profits fading.

The marketing vice president urged his boss to diversify into synthetics. The company was in a fine position to do so, he argued. Its quality reputation was established. It had a good staff of engineers and technologists, and a capable marketing force. All the company had to do was find some new suppliers and revise certain production techniques.

The president's verdict: "Not interested."

He was convinced that the turn to synthetics was a passing phase that would run its course. Key executives disagreed and left. Customer price resistance grew. Sales continued to decline. It reached a point where even the president conceded that some kind of innovation was called for. But he stubbornly refused to buy the switch to synthetics.

Instead he attempted to breathe new life into the organization by revamping the service department, changing advertising agencies, making a variety of product changes. However well intended, the innovation campaign was doomed to failure. The fact was that synthetics were easier to machine and cheaper to produce. Product durability was no problem, and results were more consistent. As the marketing vice president stated when he finally resigned, "All the innovation in the world isn't going to change these simple facts. It's like trying to drink Jello through a straw."

In the end, the innovation failed along with the company.

THE "PROBLEMATICAL APPROACH"

Some presidents who wear the Pioneer's Hat take it off when they leave the factory. Innovation, in my view, should know no bounds. It should extend far beyond product development and research. It is as applicable in the office as the plant, in the warehouse as the field. I find that in many companies pinpointing areas in need of innovation is almost as challenging as coming up with the improvement ideas. Experience has taught us that where the "problematical approach" is used, the areas of prime need tend to reveal themselves. After zeroing in on the problem, you can get down to the serious—and often lonely—business of applying talented imagination to the situation at hand. Here, drawn from a variety of operating areas, are successful examples of the kind of innovation I have in mind.

- **New products (North American Rockwell)**

Problem—To help clothe more economically the 600 million people of our world today who are estimated to be poorly and inadequately dressed.

Solution—A new high speed shuttleless loom perfected by Draper Corporation, the nation's largest producer of textile machinery.

Result—The looms are 50 percent more productive than conventional models. They will substantially reduce fabric costs. We think they will help meet the pressing needs of the world's population and at the same time produce new markets for the company.

- **Merchandise shipment (Consumer products company)**

Problem—To reduce the quantity of merchandise damaged in transit. This was costly both in dollar loss and customer dissatisfaction.

Solution—For months the company had been concentrating on stronger product components, better packaging, etc. Finally a new approach was suggested. Wood blocks and wedges formerly used to hold merchandise secure while in transit were replaced by inflatable dunnage bats.

Result—Handling flexibility was increased, labor costs reduced, merchandise damage cut more than 30 percent.

- **Maintenance (North American Rockwell)**

Problem—It took two men to service and repair a heavy piece of equipment in one of our smaller plants. One Sunday two maintenance men were called in to complete a special priority job so that production could start Monday morning. Only one man showed up.

Solution—After pondering the problem, he built a crude jig which doubled as the missing employee's pair of arms.

Result—The job was done by one man instead of two, and from this point on the jig was adapted as a regular feature, speeding the repair and cutting the labor cost. This is a prime example of the problematical approach in action. But why wait for emergencies to create inventions? With probing and analysis, you can pinpoint situations of this type which might never be otherwise revealed.

● **Absenteeism (Insurance company)**

Problem—In spite of strictly enforced discipline and publicity campaigns designed to reduce absence, the problem was growing increasingly acute.

Solution—A "carrot" strategy was employed to supplement the "stick." The company conducted a raffle with attractive prizes offered. Employee eligibility to participate depended on attendance—one raffle ticket for each month of perfect attendance.

Result—Absence reduction of 23 percent during the life of the program.

● **Factory procedures (North American Rockwell)**

Problem—To reduce machine down time.

Solution—Switch to larger rolls of wire.

Result—Down time cut 11 percent, proving that even the simplest and most obvious improvement strategies are easily overlooked unless exposed to the searching eye of a "pioneer" with problem-solving on his mind.

● **Packaging (Food producer)**

Problem—To reduce the product cost and price of a powdered product packed in individual envelopes.

Solution—An alteration from center seam to side seam was made in the product envelope.

Result—20 percent more envelopes produced on each run.

● **Salvage (Machinery producer)**

Problem—To extend the life of worn machine parts. Formerly, worn machine parts were either salvaged by a chrome plating process or scrapped. Either alternative was expensive.

Solution—Worn parts are now built up with the use of a brazing torch.

Result—Labor and material costs slashed; machine down time reduced.

● **Communications (Paper products manufacturer)**

Problem—To cut down on the high cost of bi-monthly sales summit meetings. Key executives from six major cities were brought together to review problems and revamp strategy. Travel and hotel costs were high. It was also becoming increasingly difficult because of customer commitments for all key men to get away at the same time.

Solution—Bi-monthly meetings (except semiannual) replaced by telephone conference calls.

Result—Meeting costs drastically reduced; communications flexibility increased.

The point is worth repeating. Innovation, effectively implemented by the problematical approach, need know no bounds —other than the imagination of the creative individuals engaged in the improvement effort.

SYSTEMATIZE YOUR SEARCH

Being warmly receptive to fresh ideas is not in itself sufficient to set a dynamic innovation program into motion. Experience indicates that the surest way to spark initiative is by means of a planned program that will ensure the generation of ideas, not by accident, but by design. It is the job of the president to see to it that such a program gets under way. It is his responsibility to make things happen.

Says *Management Consultant,* a quarterly bulletin issued by the Association of Consulting Management Engineers:

> ... innovations need not be the accidental, irregular things they have been in the past. By a new emphasis on research, by systematizing innovation—industry and government now make regular provision for the occurrence of new and unpredictable developments.

Here are five key techniques that have produced fruitful results in many companies. Hopefully, they will touch off program ideas for you as well:

1. Establish individual responsibility for innovation

Provide the incentive for managers and supervisors on all levels to "think smart." And provide the direction and resources which even the smartest of managers require. Define innovational objectives. Spell out specific areas of exploration. Set up a system of reporting and review to keep track of progress made. Make sure managers know that their personal growth will depend largely on the innovative contributions they produce.

2. Give research the emphasis it merits

Research activity should be geared to specific company goals and needs; these, of course, should take in all areas of consideration ranging from social responsibility to the creation of new markets. Competitive strategies in particular should be made to determine that research resources are being applied on schedule and according to plan on a pioneering, not a foot-dragging, basis.

As one president remarked to me recently: "The mark of the true pioneer is his unwillingness to merely follow the leader. Only when he knows that his company is pacing the field is he really happy."

3. Allow sufficient time for creative reflection

Too many talented managers, I find, are too busy to think. This makes about as much sense as hiring a race horse to pull a dray wagon. I know that my own personal idea output would be severely curtailed if I did not systematically allocate certain time in each week for uninhibited and unrestrained mental rambling. I particularly like to ponder problems while en route in the air with no telephones, secretaries, or meetings on tap to interrupt my thoughts. I arm myself with a series of problems and questions to mull over and see what comes out by the time we land.

Questions will vary, of course, depending on your particular problems and areas of interest. A few unrelated subjects that come to mind: What new markets can we explore for Product X that we are not presently tapping? How can we breathe new life into dormant accounts? What incentives can we offer to get key men to take training on their own time? What new techniques can we use to recruit talented scientists and engineers? What special problems can we get the computer to solve? Are we scrapping any items that might be re-used or converted into cash?

The list could go on indefinitely. The trick is to get started.

As Emerson said, "Thought is the property of those only who can entertain it."

4. Keep on top of developments in the field

The idea is not to do this on a haphazard, sometime basis. Select competent managers and charge them with the specific responsibility of keeping the company up to date. Develop an auditor's type program to assure that all areas of profit interest are covered. Review government patent sources, all types of press coverage, information exchanged at meetings of trade associations and professional societies. Keep a sharp eye via field reports and other news media on competitive innovations—service, technology, customer and community relations, image building, sales building, the entire gamut.

For example, a producer of automotive products used in the gas station trains attendants to get more mileage, more sales, more profits out of the items. A silicones manufacturer and a label producer both run customer contests with prizes awarded for unique and useful product applications. The advertising and marketing information that results pays many times over for the contest investment. A wood products company runs employee contests with the same objectives in mind. How might these programs be applied to boost your company's profit performance?

Leave such exploration to chance and scores of good ideas will elude you. Set up special provisions to track down successful ideas and programs in force, and your batting average will be a good deal higher.

5. Broaden the perspectives of your key people

Expose your managers and supervisors to problems outside their day-to-day experience. Encourage idea exchange among key people of different departments. Invite them to participate to a greater extent in higher level communications sessions. Broaden the scope of their decision-making action and authority.

Consult your key people on problems not relating directly to their own jobs It is an effective way to start rusty think wheels turning. And it is extremely flattering to a man to have his superior come to him on an equal footing for advice. It widens his horizons. It makes his job more interesting.

The main point is this. The human tendency even among

talented people is to settle comfortably into ruts of repetitive rote activity. Building a network of counter-routinization into your system will free a manager's imagination from the anchor of his daily operation.

SCOUT FOR SYMPTOMS OF CORPORATE SENILITY

Edmund Burke once said:

> If a great change is to be made in human affairs, the minds of men will be fitted to it; the general opinions and feelings will draw that way. Every fear and hope will forward it; and they who persist in opposing this mighty current will appear rather to resist the decrees of Providence itself, than the mere designs of men. They will be not so much resolute and firm as perverse and obstinate.

To some degree perversity and obstinacy exist in every organization. Usually they are well masked, even to the perverse themselves. The trick of the pioneering president is to set into motion machinery for spotting the symptoms of corporate senility and squelching the adherents of status quo-ism. The signs are not difficult to pinpoint.

Idea strangulation

Do ideas die too easily in your company, without any fuss, without any noise, without any protest?

Unholy alliances

Is innovation ever stifled by managers who sacrifice the company good for what has been termed party loyalty?

Rulebook administration

Does a too rigid adherence to protocol and directives cause programs and ideas to be stymied and stalled?

Rubberstamp management

Is the play-it-safe philosophy so deeply ingrained in your people that the imaginative maverick gets too easily slapped down?

Flowering deadwood

Do passive non-contributing managers, because of their seniority entrenchment, flourish to the same degree as dynamic driving executives who initiate new programs and ideas?

Undocumented rejection

Are ideas shelved without full documentation explaining why they were shelved, proving the impracticality of the ideas, and discussing constructive alternatives?

Unconditioned surrender

Is change so rare in certain sections of your company that people, unconditioned to adjust to the process, regard innovation as a threat to security and resist it as a matter of course?

Talent drain

Has there been an exodus of talented (and presumably frustrated) "comers" from your company?

Smug superiority

Do you have managers who consider themselves so experienced, so well informed, so downright superior, that they cannot benefit from the counsel and experience of others?

Decision paralysis

Does it take too long for important decisions to be made? Is there a tendency to shirk decision-making responsibility, or to shift it to a committee?

There are some of the major symptoms of corporate senility. Their presence militates against the success of innovation programs. The faster you identify them and grind them under your heel, the faster the machinery of progressive change will begin to operate in your company.

EXTEND YOUR PIPELINES

Innovation comes most readily to the president who exposes his mind—and his people—to the widest number of idea sources. By systematically extending your mental pipelines, you can minimize innovation by happenstance, and cause it to occur through planning and programming.

A part of one president's planning is frequent conversation with new people both inside and outside the company, a continuing exposure to fresh viewpoints. Recently this chief executive and a committee of aides had been wrestling with a difficult and important decision. It was close to resolution when the president announced, "I'm going to defer final judgment on this for one more day. The same people have been noodling it for too long. We may have gone stale." He went out and discussed the problem with someone he respected who had a totally different perspective. That same day he came back with the final decision, but it was radically different from the one that had been all but resolved.

Where can you go for a fresh perspective or the kind of thinking that will stimulate your own imagination? In the Small Business Administration's Management Aid titled *Innovation: How Much Is Enough?*, Harvard Business School editor Edward L. Anthony suggests a dozen different idea reservoirs well worth tapping by the would-be innovator:

1. Employees

Encourage them to suggest ways of improving your products, your production methods, and your marketing.

2. Customers (existing and prospective)

Ask them what they like and dislike about your product—or your method of doing business. Their opinions may give you a clue to a profitable development.

3. Suppliers

Find out trends in your business from your suppliers. Often, they can give you ideas on new materials, new machinery, and new styles.

4. Trade and technical journals

Many of these publications give examples of new ideas that have paid off. The leading publications in your field should be scanned regularly for ideas that can be adapted to your situation.

5. Trade associations

Some of these groups sponsor organized efforts to turn up and test innovations in their particular sphere of interest. You should know what, if anything, is being done in your line.

6. Learned societies

If your business is one based on hard-science technology, such as physics or chemistry, it may be very much worthwhile to follow what is being discussed in groups like the American Chemical Society, the Institute of Radio Engineers, and others.

7. Colleges and universities

Professors can often give wise advice and guidance. Don't underestimate their practical knowledge of business problems. And don't shy away from them just because you're not much of a "book man" yourself.

8. Government agencies

Research conducted or financed by the Federal Government often can be adapted to the manufacturer's need for new ideas —especially in the area of cost-cutting improvements in machinery.

9. Advertising and sales clubs

Members of these usually deal in marketing innovations of one kind or another. They can be good thought-starters.

10. Conventions

Larger gatherings bring together speakers, exhibitors, demonstrations, and attendees who share some skills but have, in addition, a wide diversity of viewpoint and occupation.

11. Civic organizations

These groups are composed, to a large extent, of business and professional people with whom ideas about possible innovations can be exchanged if trade secrets are not involved. Attendance at their meetings may not have much direct measurable pay-off, but you cannot afford to overlook the potential long-run value.

12. Libraries

Some libraries have good business sections and alert librarians who can help you get material through interlibrary loans once you have a specific line of inquiry in mind.

Cherish dissatisfaction

The customer, employee, or supplier who is blissfully content with the status quo may serve as balm for the ego. But you won't learn much from him about what you should be doing better or differently. A consultant friend told me recently, "There's a tendency among some top executives to surround themselves with sunshine spreaders. The chronic optimist has his definite value, but you've got to look at the shadows too. That's how you find out what's most in need of attention."

"Looking at shadows" is this man's occupation. He has a special talent for unearthing criticism and complaint. Often, he says, the fellow who gripes about the hop that the ball took, does so only because he dropped it. But, more frequently than most managers think, complaints point the way to areas where innovation is called for.

He calls to mind a distributor whose industrial supplies business suddenly started to fall off for no apparent reason. It took painful investigation to reveal the aggravating cause of the sales drop. To accommodate order-processing convenience, order blanks had been revised into a complex and unwieldy form. The items were low in cost, fairly standard, and available from a variety of sources. Consequently, rather than struggle with the cumbersome forms, purchasing department clerks simply switched suppliers. It took reversion to a simplified form and an expensive promotional effort to get the ship back on course. Had not the complaints of the clerks been finally uncovered through patient and persistent probing, the cause of the sales drop might never have been uprooted.

GET AWAY FROM IT ALL

In my experience, getting away from familiar environments is an excellent way to stimulate fresh ideas. Ideas multiply through association. The more varied and different the association, the more unusual the ideas.

The trick, I find, is to develop the habit of permitting problems to germinate in your mind. If you do this, the proper association will trigger the ideal solution at any time or any place. As often as not, when solutions stubbornly resist your best efforts, a change of scene will bring them to the surface.

I can recall a troublesome problem of some months' duration that was solved in minutes while on safari in Africa. I can recall an important new product idea that came to me on a business trip to Brussels. I can recall a conversation with a Tokyo businessman and a Norwegian minister in Rio that gave me the direction I was seeking in the marketing of a new customer service. Getting away from familiar surroundings and accustomed routines adds a fresh dimension to your imagination.

I know a man who runs a famous hotel chain. One day his accountants told him that business was slipping. He spent days talking across tables with management consultants and members of his staff. A lot of theories were held forth, but little in the way of constructive and imaginative innovation. My friend finally called a halt to the proceedings. He took off on a three-week jaunt to Europe and the Middle East, spending each day at a different hotel. When he came home, he had a bagful of intriguing ideas in tow. Many of them were adapted to revamp and rejuvenate programs in his own organization.

CASH IN ON YOUR COMPUTER

Information generates new thinking, and I know of no management tool for generating information that is as powerful as the computer.

The day may not be far off when those who analyze business failures will add another cause to the list—failure to adequately exploit the computer. I believe that this tool, together with the advanced techniques of business management, can open the door to an unlimited number of innovational possibilities.

The key is the systems expert, the trained specialist who can systematize a fantastically increasing body of knowledge and focus on the essential needs of society and business.

In this age of accelerating change, there are powerful forces at work that will enable corporations to achieve objectives that were heretofore unthinkable. Properly employed, the computer can help you to pinpoint and cash in on these forces.

Already, for example, the marriage of numerical control, the digital computer, and machine tools is a reality. It is one of the stunning technological innovations of our time, comparable in significance to the advent of nuclear power. In the aerospace industry, numerical control applications are being broadened to a multitude of other uses beyond the cutting of metal. These include, or will include, material handling, assembly, welding, fabrication, inspection, quality control, computer graphics, drafting machines, and plotters. And all of these individual applications are being absorbed into the systems concept of numerical control.

This is only the beginning, a small sampling of what is to come. How imaginatively is your computer being used? It is a question well worth pondering.

DREDGE UP OLD IDEAS

Countless ideas die prematurely in industry each year. But most of them are not totally destroyed. More often they are buried alive. In many cases they can be dredged up, de-tombed, and patiently restored to life.

In one company a team of consultants worked four weeks to set up a stock-picking system before a manager in another division got wind of the project. "When I was in that division I had three men working two months on that setup," he told his boss. "We made an elaborate proposal, but the idea was shelved."

The manager pulled a fat folder of papers from a dead file. Seventy percent of the consultants' work had been duplicated.

The point is clear. A mint of untapped ideas may be on hand today in your company. Almost every manager I know has his reservoir of pet projects that never got off the ground. It might pay for you to urge your key people to dig deep into dust-covered files (and drawers and shelves) for abandoned ideas they feel worthy of freshening. You never know. A proposal that produced yawns two or three years ago might fire up enthusiasm and profit growth today.

USE CONSTRUCTIVE CONFLICT TO HONE IDEAS

As R. Donald Daniel, a McKinsey & Co. principal, writes in *Dun's Review:* "Plans and ideas that haven't been subjected to challenge and criticism within the company before they're put into effect are going to be awfully vulnerable to the challenge of competition and the realities of the market place once they're implemented; the pace and complexity of business today make criticism and challenge indispensable to the development of sound corporate strategy."

On the other hand, too many ideas expire because they are debated to death. Experience teaches us that progress is born out of conflict. Yet conflict can be either constructive or degenerative, depending on the environment that is established. The trick is to control the conflict so as to sharpen rather than smother worthwhile ideas.

There is nothing so sad as seeing the demise of a good idea due to dissent. The most talented innovator of all is the executive who is capable of riding the tide of dissent without permitting it to pull him under. The area of nuclear power and progress provides a good example. Today this field is moving along at an ever-accelerating pace. Before too long we will see the development of a reactor that will produce more fissionable fuel than it consumes, at the same time that it is producing usable electric power.

North American Rockwell's Atomics International Division is deeply involved in the Breeder Reactor Program on a long-term basis. We have been working for two decades with liquid sodium, and this now turns out to be the ideal coolant and heat transfer medium for the breeder reactor. We know now that the reactor is technically feasible. We believe it will be commercially practical well before our economic need for it becomes critical in the mid-1980's. With the realization of the breeder reactor, the spectre of dwindling fuel resources will be a thing of the past.

But progress of this kind was not easy to come by. I can well remember the criticism leveled at the nuclear program in the late 50's and early 60's. The program was moving too fast. It was moving too slow. It was hurting the coal industry. It was dangerous. It was costing too much, and the money should be diverted to other efforts. Electricity from nuclear power plants was no better than electricity from conventional plants. And so on, ad infinitum.

The conclusion is obvious. Had the planners and pioneers permitted it, the tidal wave of opposition could have drowned the innovation. It points up the great need, I think, for progressive companies to find practical ways to keep conflict and opposition properly in check.

There is a critical need in business today for managers of vision and character. These men should be able and willing, on the one hand, to state their position and eloquently register their dissent as the need arises. On the other hand, they should stand ready to subordinate their dissent once marching orders are given, whether the orders are to their liking or not.

Drawing this delicate working balance is in part an educational undertaking. For one thing, managers should be made to understand the vast difference between the man who simply advocates an idea, and the man with the responsibility for the consequences to himself and to others if the idea is put into being. In my experience, I have observed that the more responsibility a man has to assume himself, the more understanding he will have of decisions made by his superior.

Programmed action is needed in corporations—as in international negotiations—to keep spirited dialogue from bogging down and ideas from being "temporarily shelved" into oblivion. If an idea is rejected, documented agreement by all parties should be produced stating the reasons for rejection in hard-nosed terms that are backed by dollar and cents evidence. Some companies I know use impartial intermediaries in an effort to bring fledgling ideas into fruition. The sole function of these referees is to keep programs moving along in the face of conflict and opposition.

It is a noble purpose, I think. Napoleon Hill once referred to ideas as "the beginning points of all fortunes." They are far too precious and far too rare to be riddled to death during skirmishes in the never-ending war on status quo-ism.

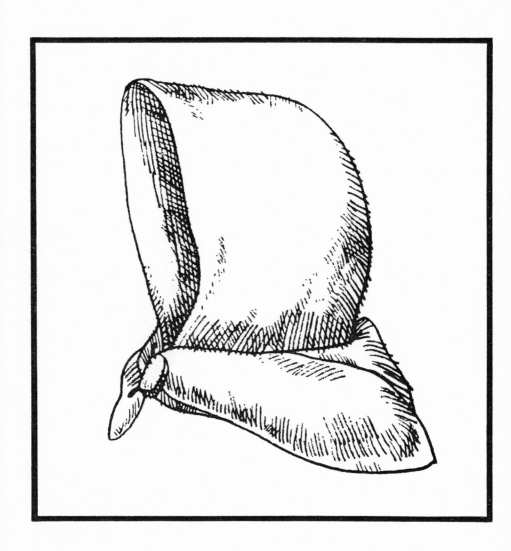

CHAPTER THREE

The Hat of the Soothsayer

The world's most famous sooth-sayer probably didn't wear a hat. I am speaking, of course, about the grim old chap who kept calling out to Julius Caesar, according to Shakespeare, "Beware the ides of March." Most ancient Romans went bareheaded, so the soothsayer probably had no hat. But the chances are good that he had the hood up on his toga —not to guard against inclement weather, but to cloak himself in mystery.

All forecasters, from the oracle of Delphi to the roadside "palmist-adviser," try to create an air of mystery: it's their stock in trade. But I sometimes wonder if their trade is so mysterious after all.

To take a frivolous example, let's examine a passage from a very modern viewer-of-the-future, Mr. Criswell of "Criswell Predicts":*

> I predict that tempers will flare in the House of Lords over a very private royal scandal . . . I predict that Richard Nixon will make history in the White House and will bring about much-needed reforms . . . I predict that in the 1970s there

---

* Criswell, *Criswell Predicts to the Year Two-Thousand* (Anderson, S.C.: Droke House Co., 1968).

will be nine states boasting of a woman governor . . . I predict that beyond a shadow of a doubt, one of the worst of all Hollywood scandals will explode on your front pages with the most sordid of details!

To examine these fearless forecasts, three out of four are extremely safe guesses. Tempers occasionally rise in all houses of government. All U.S. presidents "make history" and put reforms into effect. As for the Hollywood scandals—when *aren't* they exploding on some front page?

Now look at the item about woman governors. The exact number, of course, is a wild guess, but in essence the prediction could be called accurate because it correctly gauges a *trend* in U.S. political and economic life—the increasing participation of women. In fact, all these predictions—or soothsayings, if you will—are based on *trends*, new or continuing.

And that, of course, is what soothsaying is all about.

"The major benefit of having relatively long-range forecasts is to give you a feel for trends, not to provide exact substantive information," the president of Associated Spring Corporation, Wallace Barnes, said recently. "It is not an end in itself; it is part of the overall planning process."

Mis-guessing on some random statistic isn't too important. But mis-reading on a broad trend important to your business can be disastrous. It can send your stock plummeting and invite a takeover by some cold-eyed corporate raider. And make no mistake about it: forecasting is, in the final analysis, the president's job. To paraphrase Harry Truman, the soothsaying stops here.

HERE'S HOW IT'S DONE

Drawing on his knowledge, experience, and instincts, and on the advisory and technological resources of his company, the chief executive must be able to gaze into the future and read signs that other men might miss. Then he must act decisively and courageously to ride out the trends and surge forward, instead of being rocked by their unexpected force.

History proves that the Soothsayer's Hat can shape the destiny of a company—or a president. It's not a one-man job, but it is the president who must see to it that the job gets done. He must keep abreast of developments in all major areas of the company on an up-to-the-minute basis. He needs to know, for example, which products and services are paying their way—and which will still be paying their way three, five, and eight years hence.

Example

When the Food and Drug Administration set up minimum daily requirements for nutrition and vitamins for breakfast, manufacturers of cereals and beverages quickly brought out a variety of new products which had immediate acceptance. But the foresighted food and food additive companies looked forward to the time when the FDA would set up minimum requirements for lunch and dinner. At this writing that is still to come. But companies that fail to plan for it risk being left in the dust.

Another example

A Cincinnati wholesaler instructed his salesmen to spend several hours a week doing missionary work in a particular upriver town on the Ohio. It was a small town without much current volume potential, and competitors scoffed. But the wholesaler knew that a large utility was located there and shrewdly estimated that as years went on, the utility would assume a larger and larger burden of taxes. This would mean that the town would be an attractive place to live because ordinary citizens would have to pay significantly fewer taxes than people in nearby towns.

In six years the town began to grow like Topsy. And this wholesaler, with the ground well-prepared, had the inside track in all the retail outlets in his field.

The signs are often not too hard to read. The problem is getting a look at them. The president's pipelines must extend both within and without the corporate confines. I find it vitally important to keep a global network of fingertip sources of information available anytime of the day or night. As rumors and feelers grow into crises, I never know when crucial facts will be needed to arrive at on-the-spot decisions.

In wearing the Soothsayer's Hat, timing is essential. More than one computer producer, for example, has poured vast sums into research only to find his machines obsolete by the time they are ready for market. I have tried, in my own crystal-gazing, to take this factor properly into consideration.

Elsewhere I will discuss the way the goals of Rockwell-Standard and North American Aviation seemed to dovetail neatly, in that crucial period just before the merger that was to form North American Rockwell Corporation. There was certainly a bit of presidential prognostication in both companies. For my part, let me say now that Rockwell-Standard read the signs and concluded that we wanted to become a major factor in the field of space-age technology, but that gaining the needed expertise by acquiring a number of small companies would take too long—perhaps 20 years. And my advisors, my pipelines and my instincts alerted me to the danger that this would bring us to the station after the train had pulled out.

But more of that later.

UNCLOAKING THE SOOTHSAYER

Let's get back to Shakespeare's soothsayer and his "Beware the ides of March." Clairvoyance? Not at all. My guess is that the sly old seer had been hanging around that "street near the Capitol" and had overheard Cassius, Casca and Company plotting in their iambic pentameter. The date, March 15, was logical because of the progression of public events in Rome. Today a soothsayer might sidle up to a chairman of the board and murmur: "Beware of the next meeting of the ICC" or "Look out for the Senate Hearings."

The first thing to understand about amazing predictions, then, is that most of them aren't amazing at all. You can make them, too, if you will do the spadework.

Some soothsaying is amazing only because it's so easy. Did you know, for instance, that you can make instant projections of market potential just by running your eye down the Budget Bureau's handy Standard Industrial Classification Manual? The SIC code is a simple four-digit description of a company's major business. The first two numbers tell the general lines, such as non-electric machinery, and the next two pin it down more specifically.

Many executives use the SIC manual to define present markets. What they don't realize is that they can be real soothsayers on potential markets just by looking at the Manual and comparing it with the Bureau of the Census' "County Business Patterns," which groups companies with the same SIC number according to county and state and also gives the number of employees in each firm. And, of course, you can similarly use the SIC code to spot competition that you didn't know about—and to gather more detailed information in the almost countless government and private publications that now use SIC numbers.

All right, that's one easy route to second sight. It's one of many often overlooked management tools. But don't get the idea that *all* soothsaying is easy. Like everything else in a top job, most of it is hard work.

"My experience has taught me that the harder one works, the 'luckier' he is apt to get!" said L. F. McCollum, chairman of Continental Oil Company. So if you expect to make lucky guesses, plan to put in a large amount of sweat.

To mix a metaphor, a soothsayer must be, first of all, a good pipefitter.

PIPELINE NUMBER 1: THE WORLD OF POLITICS

Do you have at least one person in Washington whom you can call to just talk things over, find out some of the latest rumors and gossip? If you head an industrial enterprise, you should.

Maybe he's on your payroll; maybe not. Perhaps your "man in Washington" is an old business associate or friend you've kept up with over the years. He helps you out when he can and you do the same for him. Whoever he is, you should feel free to call on him as often as you like to get an opinion, or, when the need arises, an introduction to some commissioner or other official whose assistance you might need.

As a company grows it needs more and more contacts in Washington and in foreign capitals to help the president take care of its many interests. And, of course, you also need to know people at the state capital, at city hall, and in county courthouses. Better face it now.

The head of one company told me that he had been talking with a Washington lawyer about some patents, when the lawyer happened to mention that it appeared a certain large conglomerate was going to have to spin off one of its acquisitions. Antitrust pressure! This surprised my friend because there had been no published reports of the action, and it also intrigued him. He saw that the division, if it was spun off, would fit like a glove in his own diversification program.

Using the good offices of a number of third parties, he began secret negotiations with the conglomerate—long before any other potential buyers knew anything about it. The result was a profitable acquisition at reasonable cost—and no struggle.

POLITICIANS AND PREDICTIONS

When a new administration takes over on any level of government, the rumors about policy fly thick and fast. You can read columns of them every day in the papers and magazines. Of course most of the guesses are necessarily wrong. Walter Lippmann put it this way in early 1969:

> . . . No newspaperman that I can think of foresaw on Inauguration Day what Herbert Hoover or Franklin Roosevelt or John Kennedy or Lyndon Johnson would do. There is no binding connection between the words of a candidate in the campaign and the acts of the President when he is in the White House. . . . So I do not know what President Nixon will do. . . .

One way you can get a pretty good idea, however, is to check the appointments of key men—and not just on the federal level. Sure, you followed the Cabinet appointments and went over the records of each man; you tried to determine whether there would be any effect on your business. But what do you know about, say, the deputy major in your own home town? If you're like most businessmen, the answer is probably "little or nothing," and this applies to other local officials responsible for carrying out vital policy. Correct?

Here's an example. A small manufacturer was thinking of building a new plant in a town in Virginia. Since his process uses considerable water, he wanted permission from the town council to dig his own wells, rather than using and paying for town water. Because of that, he waited six months before moving on the project. The reason? He wanted time to enlist the support of the local newspaper and others interested in bringing industry to the area, rather than letting it stagnate.

By the time he actually came before the council with his proposals, most opinion leaders were on his side. Nothing supernatural about that kind of political soothsaying.

PIPELINE NUMBER 2: ECONOMICS AND YOUR COMPANY

There's no mystique about this, either. The basic techniques of the economist are simple enough. For instance, the number of people to be employed in 1980 can be very closely estimated because just about all of them have already been born, and the black art of the actuary indicates how many will die or otherwise leave the work force. You as president don't have to know exactly how these things are determined but it does help to have a rough idea.

You must realize, of course, that such data is subject to considerable error. In recent years, to take one example, young people began to marry later. Thus both the birth rate and the formation of households slowed down, requiring economists to revise their projections for the 1970s. One chief executive I know, whose company makes consumer products, almost blew his top last year when he found his forecasters using statistics that were out of date, and thus over-optimistic. He himself had noted the puzzling decline in household formations through an article he happened to read in the *New York Times*.

"It just shows a president has to keep on top of everything," he says. "I have an idea our forecasters aren't going to make the same dumb mistake any time soon, but just the same I now make it a point to run my eye down all the yearly predictions that concern our industry. Every trade magazine has its own, as well as general business magazines, investment counselors, and other sources. All I do is keep generally informed on what the economists are saying so I'll know when and if I should question the figures I get from our people."

Again, as president you must know general trends—not necessarily the weight and dollar value of the product you will move in the Minneapolis district in March, 1984. Our people pin it down pretty close in some of our divisions, of course. The vice president of marketing in the automotive division has his people out constantly looking at various factors, such as roadbuilding, that would affect our business. But there are some broad general areas that would be important to almost any business.

Among the vital economist and general business trends that should be kept track of in just about any industry, during the next decade or so, I would list these:

1. The rate of technological "fall-out" from the space, oceanography, and other exotic programs

By all accounts, more and more products useful on earth are being generated from these programs, and the company that can't find a way to share in this wealth may fall hopelessly behind in some fields. Health products, for instance, have already been revolutionized.

2. Patterns in government spending

How much money can be diverted from the Defense budget if there are no wars to fight? And will it be spent on space programs, urban renewal, or what? And how fast will the spending "action" shift from federal to state and local levels?

3. Population patterns

The question of household formations that we were talking about is only one of a couple of dozen key population factors that must concern all company presidents in any industry. The others include the employment rate, the fast growth of younger age brackets, the rise in education, the possible worldwide spread of birth control, and so much more.

4. The global stance of American enterprise

If U.S. global initiative really comes to surpass that of the local people in other parts of the world (as Europeans, for instance, fear), what will that mean to your markets? To balance of payments? To the supply of executive talent—and the very structure of the business society as we know it?

5. Will the cost of doing business continue to zoom upward?

The National Association of Manufacturers speculates that the salaries of many professional employees will double by 1984, and one labor relations professor (Dr. F. F. Feltman of Cornell) looks for unions to be bargaining during the '70's for dental and emotional health care, retirement at 55, longer vacations, portable pensions, and even guaranteed lifetime employment. And the average week, of course, continues to decrease and is expected to fall below 40 hours in the mid-'70's.

6. Will economic forecasting become truly scientific?

At the moment there are all sorts of experiments with mathematical models of national or regional economies, with the computer spewing out the answers to the eternal question, "What would happen if . . . ?" The science of the mathematician, armed with a computer, is awesome indeed. And who can say that some day these things won't be quite predictable? Another thing for you to keep track of.

7. What will be the long-range effects of the "conglomerate" trend?

More than half of *Fortune*'s 500 leading companies can be considered "conglomerates" in the sense that they include unrelated businesses under one corporate umbrella. The trend seems almost certain to continue. What will it mean in each individual industry? What about the weaker conglomerates that fall by the wayside? What completely unexpected new field might you one day find yourself operating in?

If those aren't enough to keep you awake at nights, what about soothsayers who insist that the corporation itself is "not the ideal productive unit for the coming society," as one of them put it? What about the replacement of business with a society run by scientists, with no feeling for or interest in the marketplace? Far fetched? It's being talked about this minute, in perfect seriousness, by well-informed people.

Which means, among other things, that you can't content yourself just with economic soothsaying, but must take stands and try to bring about the future you feel would be best not only for your company and your industry, but for the world in general. No small chore. I can tell you.

Business trends don't just happen. People make them happen. If Joseph Wilson, Sol Linowitz, and their associates had believed the results of a survey taken by one large rival office machines firm in the '50's, they would have concluded that there was no market for an improved copier—and there would have been no Xerox story to excite the imagination of entrepreneurs everywhere. If the coal industry had believed the dire forecasts of the early 1960's, they would just have closed up the mines. Instead they worked with the railroads and the pipelines to find new and cheaper methods of transportation, went back to their own mines to improve basic work methods, and formed a research group to find new ways to use oil and natural gas. The result, of course, has been an industry upsurge—new records in production and productivity per miner—and daily wage rates.

The whole point of economic soothsaying is to find out what you must *make* happen.

The same applies to the larger question of the whole course of our nation's economy—and indeed our free enterprise system. Looking into my personal tea leaves, I would hazard that the American public is going to become much more economically sophisticated in coming years, and that one reason for it will be more and earlier economic instruction in our schools. At any rate, I hope so.

This is a pet subject of mine, and here is as good a time as any to have my say on it.

Right now fewer than one out of twenty high school students— and one in five college students—are exposed to even a single course in economics. Yet we expect them to take their place as citizens and consumers and to help make decisions on matters affecting their personal finances and, through their votes, our total economy. Partly because some of us businessmen have been loudly promoting the idea, educators are beginning to realize that changes need to be made.

In Elkhart, Indiana, for instance, educators are introducing simple economic concepts in the first grade. The teacher leads a discussion of Christmas presents and talks about how the students' choices are governed by family income and the desires of various members of the family. Then they visit factories and talk of how the same kinds of choices are faced by nations. And in Old Hickory, Tennessee, teenagers are coming home and pestering their grandparents with questions they got from a new economics class: "Why did you move away from the farm?" "What prices did farmers get for produce in 1910?" "What did they pay for manufactured goods?" I believe examples like this will multiply around the country, and that eventually the deplorable economic illiteracy of the public will be erased.

PIPELINE NUMBER 3: YOUR COMPETITION AND YOU

If you are a president and are correctly organized, you're sitting at the narrow end of a giant funnel of information that filters in from every pair of eyes in the company. Market situations, competitive action, taxes, environmental factors—all these and more are gathered and reported in an orderly way to headquarters. The information is used for forecasts—weekly, monthly, annually, probably a three-year internal operating forecast and no doubt a five-year or longer range forecast. It's also used to analyze week-to-week competitive action, because a great deal of that information concerns what your rivals are up to—what they're doing or planning to do, and where, and with whom.

Do you use bugs, "industrial espionage"? Not necessarily.

Your people can find out a lot about competitors just from reading newspapers and trade journals, keeping their eyes and ears open at conventions and meetings, getting brokerage reports on the rival companies, using a clipping service, combing government reports, patents, and anti-trust reports.

And in this general scouting around, important tips can be had by talking with chatty rival personnel and by noting any specialized hiring, shifts in executive authority, and unusual trips by key people. Who should do this scouting? Dr. William Copulsky of W. R. Grace and Co. put it this way:

> I don't believe you have to hire spies and pay for stolen data. My best spy would not be one with a pulled-down hat planting microphones, or rifling files. He would probably have a slight paunch, a quick smile, and a hearty handshake. He would be one of my salesman.
>
> My salesman is on the firing line. He is in touch with purchasing agents, he goes to exhibitions, to sales conferences, to my customers' plants. He knows my competitor's prices, plans, and new products. I would alert him, ask him for help, for competitor's price lists, samples, literature. . . .

The trick is to set up a system to insure that what the salesman finds out is rushed to the executive suite. Archer-Daniels-Midland is one company that has such a system. Years ago an A-D-M marketing executive told an American Management Association conference how one of his salesmen happened to notice a competitive chemicals tank wagon pulling into a service station. The salesman was well aware that he was expected to be a bit of a detective, and he knew that any information he collected was to go right to his boss who in turn sent it to the regional manager and hence to Minneapolis headquarters, by telephone or teletype if the situation were urgent.

"For several months we had been trying to estimate our competitor's volume of product X to a certain important customer," said the executive, S. R. Sheeran. "During the course of his conversation with the truck driver, the salesman made a proud reference to how well product X was moving. To his amazement the driver assumed that he and the salesman were employed by the same company and began to illustrate to the salesman just how well product X was doing by discussing the number of wagons making the run, their size and frequency, as well as plans for larger equipment."

This information was at headquarters within the hour by telephone.

Just as important as getting the information, of course, is knowing how to act on it. I suppose that's another story, but just let me mention that many companies have greatly increased their agility by setting up very small management teams that can move fast in an emergency. Typically the team consists of the president, top financial officer, a legal officer with good government contracts, and possibly an outside public relations counsel.

Specific teams are set up on paper to deal with specific kinds of brush fires from a marketing invasion to a tender offer, and it's up to the chief executive to bring the right team into play for the right situation. Or, perhaps, quickly organize a temporary task force.

All this involves complex logistical and psychological problems, not the least of which is keeping your executives interested in and working at their regular responsibilities during their periods on the special groups. And it frequently involves still another pipeline to predictions, one we've just mentioned—outside consultants.

PIPELINE NUMBER 4: YOUR CONSULTANTS

At North American Rockwell, we have one consulting company that meets with us every quarter in our operating analysis meeting. They make a presentation to us on the factors as they see them. Over the years they have been very effective, and they have continued to get closer and closer to the factors that are important to our business.

Many companies have this special relationship with one consultant, to help predict the future. At the same time you can use specialists within a particular field, such as electronic data processing, marketing, or even behavioral science.

The EDP man can predict what equipment is rapidly going to become obsolescent. He may be able to tell you when to hold out six months, in anticipation of a price drop. The marketing man can tell you what kind of sales training methods, for example, are likely to meet needs in the next few years. The behavioral scientist might be able to spot future morale problems in certain departments.

Sometimes an experienced general management consultant can spend a few months looking over an information reporting system and then advise you in no uncertain terms that unless the forms are redesigned and rerouted, there will be utter chaos when you reach a certain volume level.

No doubt about it. Consultants are valuable assistant soothsayers. Choose them with care.

PIPELINE NUMBER 5: THE SEMINAR SCENE

Did you know that Harvard's Graduate School of Business changed its curriculum at the beginning of the '60's, not to prepare its students for that decade, but to give them the skills foreseen as most important in the 1970's—a full ten years after the change was made? That, at any rate, was the announced reason for the stress on social science and mathematics. And no doubt Harvard is already re-shuffling its curriculum to get ready for the '80's.

Not many summer workshops, seminars, and night classes are as advanced as Harvard, perhaps. But just the same there is a lot of soothsaying material to be picked up in them, along with their other benefits. At best, you can play a computerized business game during some campus workshop that will help you not only to develop managerial skills but also to predict the future course of your industry. Or you might try one of the several Washington courses that tip you off to the trend of thinking in government. Or you might take a "mind-stretching" course on campus and learn to understand people better by studying great literature. Of course, seminars should be chosen carefully—many are a waste of time or an excuse to go to a desert resort in the middle of winter. To find out about courses you may not have heard of, check directories such as the technically oriented Learning Resources Directory of the Engineers Joint Council in New York. And you should choose with equal care the person from your company to attend the seminar. If he's a top executive, the president should counsel him before he goes and "de-brief" him when he returns.

At the very least, you or the man you pick to attend a course can learn some of the upcoming words or jargon that you may or may not need in the future. You may never use the word "micro-environment," for instance, or "econometric," but when you hear them they will register in your mind as something more than sheer gobbledygook.

PUTTING IT ALL TOGETHER

The object of all the forecasting, in the words of one management adviser, is simply to answer two basic questions: "Where do we want to go? How are we going to get there?"

So you look into the future. In the next year or so you foresee the need for certain equipment and a specified return on investment; you look a little further and see what new facilities will be needed in five years; and you peer further into the future and see what acquisitions, new kinds of products, and additional plants you will need to compete in an entirely different business scene. You check population trends, project long-term spending, try to determine what new kinds of managers you will need for that new technology. You try to estimate how much your marketing function will have to expand in ten years. And perhaps most important of all, you look over all predictions of the future and get a fix on the new types of products that people may want and need, and what you might do to supply them.

There's still another bit of soothsaying that can't be overstressed. How are you at predicting which of your people will burn up the track in the next few years? Who's going to be fully equipped to take over as controller or manufacturing vice president? And which man are you in danger of losing because he hasn't been challenged enough—or because he sees himself in a dead-end job?

At North American Rockwell, we try to spot the capabilities and to develop them. Just the other day, for instance, we took one of our top research men and threw him into a responsibility calling for almost straight selling. Why? Because he showed us a certain spark in conferences, in his day-to-day dealings, that indicated he might have the stuff of a generalist with wide skills. There's not a trace of marketing in his background, and hardly any administration. But he has a feel for customer needs and we think he's a leader. He's going into an accelerated exposure program over the next few years and if it works out, we won't be losing a scientist, we'll be gaining a senior executive.

The whole idea of bringing in new managers is, of course, one of the most important parts of the soothsayer's art. Will you need a different kind of technical expertise for those new products a decade from now? And will that kind of skill be available when you're ready for it, or had you better start recruiting at least five years before you actually need them? These are the questions that haunt a president.

And what of the cost? The National Association of Manufacturers tells us it costs $5000 to recruit a middle manager or professional man now (not including pay increase or loss of productiveness in first months of employment), and that it will cost $7000 in 1976 and $9000 in 1984. And recruiting costs for other jobs—your own, for instance, and that of other ranking executives—are going up even faster. About $100,000 for a top exec in 1984, says the NAM, as compared with $40,000 now.

Apart from management people, what about the great bulk of the work force? Are you taking this into consideration when you plan new plants? Of course you are. But have you checked some of the long-range population forecasts, relating them to your needs in terms of skills, age, sex of workers, etc.? How about the expected jump in population in the western desert states, or Florida? Or the new concentration of industry that is expected to develop in the heartland of the upper Mississippi Valley? And the slower but still steady growth on both coasts?

More material for midnight pondering.

OF HINDSIGHT AND HUNCHES

"After the event, even a fool is wiser," said Homer in the *Iliad*. And what's the matter with that? For years the U.S. Department of Defense has profitably used something called "Operation Hindsight" to take a cold, hard look at a weapons program in order to see how the past record can improve future projects. All events in a project are listed and then the lists for successful projects are compared with those that didn't work out so well. Then it's easy to see what was done wrong—or right.

Commented the Research Institute of America, in analyzing the program: "The key to this plan for effective hindsight is unsentimental objectivity—and that can be achieved in part by the breaking down of all the occurrence being studied into small, separate events—facts. An earnest desire to develop success patterns and to avoid failure patterns, regardless where praise or blame is deserved, will increase the chances of objectivity.

"It's still best to try to be wise before rather than after. But wisdom can be developed by the judicious use of hindsight."

Another factor not to overlook is considerably less scientific. It's simply your hunches.

The best soothsayer in the world is still guessing. Face it—and train yourself to guess. After you collect all the facts, analyze them rationally but don't be afraid to add the slightly mysterious ingredient of intuition. Pull up the hood on your toga! When "something tells you" that an event is going to work out in a certain way, try to figure out what it is that makes you feel that way.

Let your intuition take over at times. It may be highly creative whether you entirely understand the process or not.

Ever have a feeling that you didn't want to submit specs on a particular contract, that it would be a waste of time? If you thought about it carefully, you would recall that the customer in question once burned you with "engineer picking"—getting the benefit of detailed studies from several potential suppliers, but all the time planning to give the job to some cut-rate outfit that couldn't come up with that kind of study on its own.

Sometimes you have a hunch who's going to get the top spot at a company you deal with, when the chief exec retires over there. You can't put your finger on any one reason. It's just how you feel about it, on the basis of hundreds of conversations, and contacts over the years, along with your judgment of what kind of executive the company will hire, if the board knows its onions.

So listen to your hunches; try to analyze them. You may dredge up some inside information you didn't know you had.

You can prod your intuition a little if you want. One way is purposely to look at things in a new way. Suppose a certain department in your company just didn't exist, and you were going to set it up, starting from scratch. Would your new, fresh version of that department look like the real one? How would it be different—and why can't you change that department in the future to be more nearly ideal?

Here are a few other exercises to stimulate your thinking:

Pretend you're going to re-assign every manager reporting to you

Who would get which job? This gives you a sharp look at your own feelings about each man—and helps you predict his future performance.

Pretend you're going to drop all your existing products and go into completely different lines

What parts of the organization, and which people, are flexible enough to swing with such a change? And why?

Pretend uranium was found in the ground under each of your plants

What would you do with the new flow of funds? Or pretend that the company met with some gigantic and unexpected liability. What would you do to save the enterprise?

One caution. Mental gymnastics like this might improve your soothsaying. But they won't take the place of the obvious—simple curiosity. At times I find the president's role not so different from that of the gossip columnists. It's a matter of putting out the feed lines where they will do the most good. And I don't think the president can afford Thoreau's luxury of communicating with nature alone. His antennae must be tuned 365 days a year to the marts of industry as well. His trend spotters and trend analyzers should be strategically located at home, in Washington, abroad—wherever important developments are likely to take place.

Once these channels are well-established and operating smoothly, he needs just two more major elements in order to wear the Hat of the Soothsayer to the best possible advantage: a good measure of luck, and a larger measure of determination. Wrote a foods magazine editor named Charles Sirey recently:

> I predict that this year will be the best for me personally so far; I also predict that it will be the best year for this magazine and for this industry in general. The predictions are based on the personal conviction that we (the magazine, the industry and I) have the ability to make them come true.
>
> In fact, they are not so much predictions as they are decisions.

CHAPTER FOUR

The Hat of the Impresario

He's not the conductor, not the soloist nor the concertmaster. He doesn't compose. He can't dance. He's not sure what switch to pull to make the orchestra lights come on. But the concert or ballet couldn't go on without him, because he's the one who brings it all together.

He is the *Impresario*. Typically, he contracts to bring the performers to town, hires the hall, and sells the tickets. In the case of a great impresario like Sol Hurok, he does much, much more. His taste and integrity and venture capital can set the cultural patterns of a nation for decades—and he makes money at it.

The president, too, must be a mover of men and ideas. He must keep the corporate wheels at full speed constantly. They do not spin of their own accord. There must be a president who is the Sol Hurok of his company, the prime moving force of the organization. And today the Hat of the Impresario looms larger and taller than ever, simply because the challenge is greater than it has ever been before.

We are living in a seller's market. A capable and experienced manager can write his own ticket on almost any railroad. I can remember the time when a manager's main worry was: If I don't produce, I'll lose my job. This is still true, of course. But in a very real sense, the tides are reversed. The old rules of motivation no longer hold true. Money, though still an important incentive, is no panacea for managerial discontentment. Money alone will not keep a capable manager producing at peak efficiency.

Today the corporation as well as the man must carry its weight. It is the chief executive's job to provide the kind of charged environment that impels in men the urge toward self-motivation. The stimuli I am talking about are the kind that fire a manager's loyalty and pride, that spark within him a love and excitement for the role that he plays and the goals he attempts to achieve. Corny? Perhaps. But experience proves that if you cannot induce a manager to move compulsively forward on his own, he will grow edgy and restless.

The corporation that succeeds in triggering and sustaining enthusiasm among its key people is the one that winds up leading the pack. In lesser organizations your good men move out, and only the leaners remain. When this happens, take care. It is the beginning of the end.

From what source do enthusiasm, ambition, and dedicated drive derive? One thing I know for certain. They cannot be generated through the time-worn system of automatic raises and periodic promotions.

I agree completely with president Roger Sonnabend of Hotel Corporation of America when he said: "The age of the standardized raise is over. The people who perform in a superior way must have the superiority identified, acknowledged, and rewarded."

I know one corporation where almost every manager is assured regular increments, bonuses, and promotions on a year-in-year-out basis. No one will say openly that he is displeased with the arrangement. Yet I suspect that every manager there who is above run-of-the-mill calibre feels a deep and disquieting dissatisfaction in his job, even if he is unable to put it into words.

A talented manager, recently of the company just mentioned, is one of the few who did express what many of his former associates preferred to leave unvoiced.

"For two or three years," he confided, "the feeling has been building in me that the money is a kind of trap. The work is getting lifeless and dull. Maybe it's because the fight is missing. Men with jobs about equivalent to mine are getting the same recognition, even when they produce less. It's not right. I think a man should be judged on the kind of job he does, not on his ability to show up for work on time."

I couldn't agree more, and this manager knows it. Perhaps that is why he is now working for North American Rockwell. I have seen it again and again. When you give a manager raises which stem only from corporate habit or policy instead of from personal contribution, you dull his competitive instincts. You demotivate him. It is like telling Johnny he will get a hundred on the exam whether he knows the answers or not.

Managers should be rewarded, financially and intellectually, not by function but by achievement. More and more thoughtful chief executives are coming to appreciate and accept this premise. In one fast growing company that does business with us, I have seen a young executive earn more in a given six-month period than his immediate superior. The reason is that he performed outstandingly well over this time and made a particular profit contribution.

In my view a man's recognition, financial and otherwise, should be commensurate with his track record. This may shake some people up. But I think the ones disturbed will need disturbing.

TAILOR THE SUIT TO THE MAN

Some managers search hard for "motivational techniques" that work. When they find one, they delude themselves into thinking that here is something new and important that is going to boost productivity in the whole department. But the motivational strategy that works on one man may have absolutely no effect on another. Across-the-board ploys are rarely effective.

In one situation, a young assistant manager complained to his boss that he wasn't getting enough of a chance to operate independently of his chief's supervision and direction. He wanted more assignments for which he would be personally responsible, where he would be able to tackle problems and make decisions on his own.

The boss was surprised because he had not rated this man as a particularly ambitious type. In fact, repeated attempts to get him to apply creative thinking to his job had been unsuccessful.

But an opportunity did arise to try the young staff assistant on a project of his own. The assignment involved the data processing department in one division. There was a need to streamline and coordinate ordering and inventory recording procedures, pinpoint trouble spots, and work up a reporting and analysis system for followup and review.

The assistant was delighted with the assignment. He plunged enthusiastically into the effort and did an outstanding job which opened his boss's eyes to his talents and capabilities.

In the weeks ahead, the young man was given other projects on his own. The pattern repeated itself. When he worked independently and assumed sole responsibility for performance, the results were excellent. If he worked with a group, or under a superior's close supervision, his interest flagged, and performance dropped. Obviously, working on his own satisfied an important basic need for this young man. It was the motivating force that brought out his maximum potential.

His boss was elated. He felt he had gained a valuable insight into what makes people work harder and more effectively. Unfortunately, he was wrong. When he tried the same strategy on others in the department, it met with little or no success in most cases. The reason is simple.

Different people respond to different stimuli. The trick is to identify the motivational trigger that works most effectively with each individual. One man seeks additional responsibility; another shuns it. One man wants to lead; another would rather follow. One man wants to be in the limelight; another is quiet and reserved.

The idea, as an industrial psychologist puts it, is to study your man. Find out what kind of person he is. What does he want most? What moves him to action? What leaves him indifferent and unperturbed? You can never tell without probing a man's mind what the answers to these questions will be.

I recall a department manager in our employ several years ago who was a rather uninspired and uninspiring individual. He had a good legal mind and was fairly competent in his specialized area of contract negotiations. Over a period of years he had worked his way up into the lower middle management ranks, and to all apparent signs this was as far as either his ambition or capabilities would permit him to climb. In short, he was a difficult man to shake from his groove.

One day a misinterpretation of a revised company policy created a serious backlog situation in the department. Several contracts had to be restructured, and the work fell days behind. This had never happened before. Telephones hummed. Executive pressures were brought to bear. The office, traditionally one of the most tranquil, turned overnight into a hectic approximation of bedlam.

I have never seen so dramatic a change come over an individual. The emergency situation had an extraordinary impact on our customarily phlegmatic manager. He became a dynamo of action, a super-force of efficiency. His work pace quickened. He took on new life and purpose which infused itself into others. He worked out ingenious ways to cut down the backlog without sacrificing quality or thoroughness. Using a rare mix of persuasiveness and logic, he made deals to get extra help. He was transformed from one day to the next into a first-rate planner and organizer.

The reason behind it all? Apparently this manager's special motivational trigger had been accidentally tripped. He could not stand to have the normal routine disrupted. If things did not proceed in orderly fashion and according to schedule, he was unable to rest.

His boss at the time, as I recall, had been sharp enough to recognize what had happened and to cash in on it. Shortly after, the manager was put in charge of special projects, a much more dynamic and demanding job, calling for the very talents he had unexpectedly revealed. There is an ingredient of excitement and challenge to this job that the manager finds interesting and enjoyable. He loves his work as he never did before, and has since climbed to a level that nobody imagined he would reach.

It is not the only time I have seen this happen. When you find the proper motivational activator, there is no telling what new heights of achievement your man may reach.

MAKE WORK SATISFYING AND MEANINGFUL

Psychological studies conducted by AT&T and a number of other companies indicate that a job satisfaction relates, very simply, to the content of the work itself. The conclusion is obvious. The surest way to move a manager to higher levels of productivity and achievement is to make his assignments more meaningful, more interesting, more challenging.

As the English philosopher Collingwood wrote: "Perfect freedom is reserved for the man who lives by his own work and in that work does what he wants to do."

The problem, of course, is how to make an individual's work more meaningful. How can you be sure of giving him "what he wants to do"?

It is no easy task. But you can gain some measure of success by identifying the ingredients relating to a man's work which, taken together, add up to the sum of job satisfaction. This subject is discussed with considerable insight and depth by authors Herzberg, Mausner, and Snyderman in an outstanding research report called *The Motivation to Work* (John Wiley and Sons, 1959). Among the chief ingredients cited by the authors of this book and other psychologists, sociologists, and students of business, the following are of particular significance:

● **The work a person performs should provide a clear opportunity for growth**

Growth does not apply to the manager's income and status alone. It implies the opportunity to learn and broaden his mind as well, plus the chance to put his new knowledge to use in tackling problems and decisions that are intellectually stimulating. And it implies a gradual upgrading of responsibility in pace with his increasing capability to cope with complex situations and stand more independently on his own two feet.

A manager grows best, I have found, when his personal goals are closely linked, on the short run, to the growth of his group; on the longer run, to the growth of his company. It is rarely simple to dovetail or even relate personal and corporate goals, and it is my suspicion that in industry today more lip service than genuine attention is being paid to the concept of mutual growth. But of one thing I am certain. If the kind of satisfaction I am discussing is not inherent in the work a man does from day to day, no amount of money can purchase it. You can buy a man's time, but you cannot buy the man.

One point more. What about pleasure and happiness? Do they correlate well to productivity and growth? Not necessarily, say many experts. Professor Chris Argyris of Yale University, for instance, says: "To emphasize happiness and pleasure is to overlook the enormous significance of tension for self-realization. And to meet this need I believe that human relations policies will need to be significantly shifted." The stress, in short, should be not so much on what the company can do for the man, but on what you can help the man to achieve for himself.

● **The job a man does should tax his ability realistically, but to the hilt**

In a division of an electrical components manufacturer, a bright young manager was hired on the heels of a reorganization and reshuffling of personnel. Quickly spotting his ability and intelligence, his boss gave him an assignment he regarded as difficult and challenging. A few weeks later, the man resigned. He had found the work boring and dull. His boss was more surprised than he should have been. For the man who had held the job previously, the work had been stimulating. But the new manager's intellectual capacity was levels higher.

The point is this: there is no such thing as a generally challenging assignment. Work satisfaction is strongly individualized and highly personal. What churns up one man's imagination may cause another to yawn. It reverts back to the old axiom of "knowing your man." In this case a professional ballplayer was thrown into a sand lot game. Understandably he was uninspired.

● **Clarify work objectives, immediate and long range**

In certain agencies of the government the work is so highly confidential that the people doing it literally hardly know what's going on. In the particular operation I have in mind, analytical studies, before being assigned to specific personnel, are subdivided at the administrative level into a variety of parts. Each part is executed at a separate place independently of the other parts. The links set up from segment to segment are so tenuous that only the barest minimum of coordinating officers have a true picture of the overall objective and scope of the project.

The people working in this group are in the main highly creative scientists. The level of frustration is high. In a vague way those engaged in the work know it is important. But I know at least one gifted operations research analyst who resigned his well-paying job because he found the conditions of work intolerable. "I know it can't be helped," he told me, "but the job was getting me down. It was like trying to grope my way through a thick, endless forest, I had no idea where I was going or why, and what the significance would be if I ever found the clearing."

It is difficult to sustain interest in a work environment where objectives are not clearly defined. The illustration cited is an extreme case, of course. But I wonder if it is quite as extreme as some high level executives would like to believe. In large corporations especially, primary and wide-range goals sometimes tend to become obscured in the maze of secondary objectives. Scores of reports, for example, are being generated every day by people who have little understanding of how they will be used and why. As I view it, sustained interest and enthusiasm implies involvement. And involvement without complete understanding can rarely be achieved.

● **Success should be measurable and continuously measured**

"What kind of job did I do?" Whether he voices it or not, each individual finds the question one of great importance. Whatever his level, he wants to know on a regular basis how the boss is rating the job that he does. In my experience, providing such feedback for your people is an absolute essential to the development of work satisfaction. The feedback need not be highly formalized, although some degree of formalization such as periodic reviews and appraisal conferences are often helpful. But I think much of the feedback can be generated by small tokens of recognition and esteem.

Generally speaking, in a well-run group, successes outnumber the failures. But too many managers take success for granted. They operate under the premise that if their people don't hear otherwise from the boss they can assume everything is all right. I think this attitude is a mistake. Most human beings, however capable, need periodic reassurances of their ability. I have seen instances where managers, having received no word from the boss over an extended period of time regarding his appraisal of a project, conjured up all kinds of dire visions in their minds, when all along the boss was simply too busy or preoccupied to get back to the man with an expression of praise or encouragement.

In my view, one of the most serious human relations errors a manager can make is to be too busy or thoughtless to give his people the personal recognition they need and deserve. Actually, the time involved is negligible. Often a simple note will do the trick, a passing word, a phone call expressing thanks for a job well done. If a contribution is of special significance, of course, special recognition, money or praise or both, may be called for. In such cases the man's achievement should be publicized, played up as much as possible, called to the attention of others. And finally, recognition, to be most effective, should follow as closely as possible on the heels of the performance being recognized.

Patting a manager on the back for his successes is important for another purely practical reason as well. There come times in every operation where the boss must call his subordinates to account for poor workmanship or sub-par performance. It is highly demoralizing to a person if his boss calls attention only to his failures, and takes his triumphs for granted. Yet I suspect that this happens all too often in business today. Time, it seems, is forever of the essence. In the rush of daily affairs it is so easy to forget those small personal touches of appreciation which have such great meaning to the individual. I can think of no better way for a manager to invest his time, however busy he may be.

TREAT HIM LIKE A MANAGER IF YOU EXPECT HIM TO MANAGE

A manager, if he rates the title, is a professional and should be treated like one.

Some executives, in handling managerial subordinates, treat them like schoolchildren instead. I know of a marketing vice president in one company who, although otherwise capable, succeeds in stifling the imagination and growth potential of his key people with his schoolteacher approach. As a result he slows the movement, not only of managers, but of ideas as well.

To illustrate, one of his subordinates is titled manager of public relations. He does a certain amount of supervising, but very little managing in the true sense. Typically, in turning over an assignment, his superior defines the problem, outlines the objectives, then spells out what needs to be done and how to do it, step by step.

The public relations manager does not lack talent or natural intelligence. But he is young, impressionable, recently appointed, and relatively inexperienced. He follows the operating pattern set forth by his boss in good faith and without questioning it. There is only one trouble with the arrangement. He does not think for himself.

After the boss spells out the assignment, he instructs his subordinate to come to him if he runs into any problems. He even goes a step further. On a frequent and regular basis, he "follows up" on the work. And his idea of followup is to anticipate hurdles and take the initiative in cutting them down. Where important decisions are required, he does not trust the younger man to make them, so he makes them himself.

In truth, the vice president is an insecure man. In his ceaseless determination to play it safe, he makes every effort to minimize the risk of poor decisions. To a degree he succeeds. But he pays a stiff price for his fear of failure. For one thing, he develops errand boys and clerks in place of managers. A Cleveland consultant cautions strongly against this practice. "Let your people make their own decisions," he counsels, "and accept the errors of judgment they will make from time to time as part of your company's investment in management development. I think we are hearing too much these days about the so-called 'open door policy.' The fact of the matter is that if your door is open to your people every time they run up against a difficult problem or roadblock, they will be coming to you for solutions as a matter of course. This may get the immediate problem out of the way. But it will do nothing towards preparing your people for coping with a similar problem the next time around."

Another important indictment against the schoolteacher approach is its insidious effect on morale. The manager who is not permitted to stand on his own two feet soon loses faith in himself and in his managerial ability. The savvy and experienced manager who is not permitted to manage will quickly read the signs and be on his way. The lesser or greener man who remains will have his potential systematically undermined. His creative instincts will be squelched. His talents will rust through disuse. It is from a process such as this that learners and mediocrities are spawned. Men are not born mediocre. They are molded that way.

Finally, the boss who stifles his people weakens his own effectiveness as well. Any time used to perform a task, solve a problem, or make a decision that should be delegated, is time taken away from higher level activities that could and should be undertaken. In the illustration just cited, the vice president compensates for this by working long hours and toting home a briefcase over weekends. It is a pathetic way out of the dilemma. Midnight oil is no fuel on which to run a department or a business.

This vice president in question is coronary bait. He lives in great danger of running himself down, if he does not run down his operation first. For one thing, grinding away constantly on all cylinders with no time out for relaxation—or preventive maintenance, as I like to think of it—is extremely limiting on the intellect as well as detrimental to the human machine. The executive who operates in this manner may be unwittingly speeding down a dark street with a blank wall at the end.

Today a new breed of management professional is on the rise. He is a man of many interests and pursuits. He can converse intelligently on a variety of subjects. Capable as a manager, he is capable as a human being as well.

Such a manager will pull away from the shop from time to time to re-examine his values, reassess his perspectives, and re-charge his batteries. Most important, he will see to it that his department runs as smoothly and efficiently in his absence as it does when he is on hand.

Long study and experience at North American Rockwell have taught us that the best way to develop confidence, character, and skill in people, and to keep your comers coming, is to force problem solving and decision making down to the lowest possible level in the organization. It is the only way to make potential thinkers think. No executive, in my opinion, can afford to lose sight of the premise that fulfillment is an absolute essential in every manager's life and occupation. The manager who is not permitted to make his own decisions, solve his own problems, and manage his own job, cannot be fulfilled. Unfulfilled, he cannot be satisfied. Dissatisfied, he cannot succeed as a manager.

PUT DOWN THE PICAYUNE

One of America's great industrial leaders was recently characterized by an admiring associate with these words: "There isn't a chintzy bone in his body." It was a great compliment, I believe, and a significant observation.

Injecting pettiness into your dealings with your key people will take the edge off their initiative and reduce your personal stature in the process.

We are living in a dynamic and fast-moving era. It is an age of bold men and big ideas. There is no place for small-minded haggling and unreasoned pennypinching on today's high level management team. The executive who finds himself in front of the crowd is the man with the courage and vision to unflinchingly make the investment in progress that is required of him.

Does this imply a free and easy spendthrift philosophy? Anything but. In a profit-oriented enterprise costs must be properly controlled, budgets tightly administered, activities constrained within reasonable limits. On the other hand, you can't earn a dollar without spending a dollar. I have observed among many managers the tendency to become so obsessed with the cost-cutting effort that they economize opportunity and profit growth right out of existence. Mindless pennypinching can have a profoundly detrimental effect on individual performance, as can other forms of petty behavior. It can shrink a man's perspective and cause his imagination to shrivel.

Pettiness in business can take a variety of tacks, and of course it is unconsciously applied. Following are five ways to see that small-mindedness doesn't creep into your operation:

1. Let your key people control their own time

A manager deserves the faith and trust of his superior or he shouldn't be in his job. In our company the chief concern is with the man's productivity, not the way he spends his time. We shoot for specified results. How the manager achieves the results are mainly his problem, so long as he gets them. We don't check up to see whether he is regularly in the office or out of the office, at his desk or away from his desk. In short, he is pretty much in business for himself. Operating under this philosophy pays off, we find. It gives a manager the self-respect and professional bearing he needs to operate with confidence and with the long-range picture in mind. Not every organization can operate in this way, unfortunately. In order to do so, an accurate and reliable system of measurement and evaluation is required. But this is the main key to sound and profitable business operation in any case. And a valuable byproduct of reliable measurement is that it enables you to disregard the petty details and concentrate on profit performance and results.

2. Don't nitpick procedures

Effective management bears a strong similarity to good contract bridge. In bridge, the declarer can select any number of strategies to make his contract. The one he chooses is not important as long as the maximum result is obtained. In management too, the proverbial cat can be skinned in a variety of ways. But too often the seasoned executive is tempted to impose his own procedures and philosophies on his subordinates. If it happens that the "guidance" designed to save time, money, or work is too detailed, or on too low a level, the effect may be more damaging than helpful. In short, niggling nitpicking generally produces little more than annoyance and frustration.

I know that quite often, for example, I come across reports, letters, methods of operation and the like that I feel could stand improvement. And it sometimes requires genuine willpower to hold back criticism. But experience has trained me to weigh the significance of the criticism, and to pose this question to myself: "Will the improvement, if indeed improvement it is, make a real difference in the achievement of the desired result?" If the answer is no, as it usually is, I force myself to hold my tongue. It is more important, I feel, for a manager to maintain his stride and self-assurance than it is for the boss to mold the man in his image, superior or not.

3. Identify positive idea values

Ideas rarely emerge from men's minds as earth-shattering brainstorms. More often they are crudely and uninspiringly expressed. I think a manager should keep this in mind when communicating with his people.

Many executives, I find, thoughtlessly come up with an adverse reaction to the idea which, at first blush, appears to have little or no merit. That is why I regard it as good discipline to hold back on your initial response to any idea if it happens to be negative. Hear the man out. Give your mental machinery time to grind over the pros and cons. Those hard second thoughts may reveal the idea in an entirely different light. Most important, take care not to peck away at the roadblocks and objections. Concentrate on the positive values instead. If the idea has any possibility of being converted into profit action, work with the suggestor to strengthen his tottering brainchild into an entity that can stand on its own power. And don't do this by taking over or participating in the authorship. Do it rather by means of subtle thought transplants delicately applied. Your guidance and direction may be helpful indeed. But the less obvious it is, the more helpful it will be.

4. Back your convictions with cash

In a medical supply company I know of, a cost cutting campaign was operating full blast. Despite this fact, a production manager approached his boss, the vice president of manufacturing, with these words: "This may sound crazy, but I have to get it off my chest. I think I've come up with an idea that will save us more than $100,000 a year. But it will cost about $250,000 for the initial equipment outlay." What he was proposing in effect was a quarter of a million dollar expenditure in the midst of an austerity drive. Many superiors in such a situation would have scoffed the man down to size. Not this executive. "Let's hear about it," he replied. The manager spelled it out. His boss liked the idea and became convinced that it would work.

Austerity drive or not, he was determined to fight for the idea with every ounce of energy he could muster. Against stiff opposition, he succeeded in selling the plan to the board of directors. The point is clear. Rules, edicts, and the like are provided as necessary guidelines and planning tools. But they are not inviolate. Only two things in business are sacred in my book. One is morality. The other is profits. Anything that contributes to a company's profit performance, no matter how offbeat, no matter how contrary to established policy and procedure, is worth fighting for. The manager who is too easily scared off by the tides of opposition against him will let opportunities pass him by. Equally important, he will narrow the focus and horizons of his people. The manager who proves to his people that he is ready to spend big money on big ideas will develop broadening subordinates in a growth environment.

5. Reflect with pride the achievements of your people

Pettiness takes an ugly turn when the boss is in competition with his people for esteem. I can recall one executive who frequently made it a point to praise subordinates in the presence of his superiors. When it came to day-to-day actions, however, he overrode their judgments in a dozen small ways so as to spotlight his personal superiority. In short, he paid lip service to crediting his people for their ideas and contributions. But deep down he was a phony. His mind was too miniscule to understand that in the eyes of top management, the boss is a mirror of the progress and development of his subordinates. This executive did not do well with his people or perform outstandingly on his job.

The truth is that when a manager succeeds, the superior who helped in his grooming and development shares handsomely in his success. Most high-level business leaders I know today will go out of their way to disclaim credit for accomplishments where their subordinates have played an important role. They would rather heap the praise on their people. And with good reason. In some ways it benefits the boss more to have a subordinate come up with a meaningful profit action than to have initiated the idea on his own.

MASTER THE POWERFUL TECHNIQUE OF IDEA TRANSFER

A manager on the move is like a ravenous tiger that gobbles down every cut of meat tossed into the cage. The dynamic manager is just as voracious—except that his insatiability relates to profit ideas. He can't get enough of them, and sometimes it is up to the boss to see to it that his supply never diminishes.

The trick, I have found, is to keep your key people in mind throughout the business day. To switch metaphors, idea pollen is always in the air. It drifts through to the alert management mind by means of business discussions, reports, publications, telephone calls, salesmen's calls, a myriad of proposals. Opportunities are forever arising. One profit angle will concern one man, another somebody else. A third idea may concern a group of men.

Experience has taught me that the technique of idea transfer can serve as a powerful management tool. The way it works is simple. When the idea is generated, you immediately relate it and lateral it to the person or persons best equipped to strengthen it into a flourishing profit entity.

An idea doesn't have to be full blown to take to seed and sprout. Some managers might question the validity of this premise. An idea should be permitted to settle a while, they will argue, to develop and mature in the subconscious mind. I have no quarrel with this argument. But why continue idea germination to a single mind when you can get several good minds percolating away simultaneously?

There is another point in favor of this concept. Managers, I have found, enjoy sharing confidences with the boss. It is flattering to know that your superior values your opinion and relies on your thinking to develop programs and projects. I know, for example, that there is a perpetual profit conspiracy among my own top staff. It is fed in some measure by my own continuing flow of ideas. From what I have seen, as long as ideas are circulated and are transferred from mind to mind, progress is never at a standstill.

In my own operating experience, I find that ideas circulate best when you put them into writing the moment they occur. A tactic I often use is to dictate the thought in the form of a short note to Manager A or B, or both of them, with a file copy for my secretary. It may consist of only a line or two, followed by, "What do you think?" Assuming that you have developed the proper rapport and communications among your key management people, that is all that should be needed.

Finally, there is one step more to this concept of idea transfer. Generating and circulating ideas is not enough. Followup is equally important. I am sure that all of the ideas in this nation that were set forth and never acted upon would fill a good-sized ocean if one were capable of measuring them. It was the German scholar, Thomas à Kempis, who said: "When out of sight, quickly also out of mind." It is the boss's responsibility to assure that ideas, once proposed, are kept constantly in forward motion.

A good manager is like the proverbial elephant. He should never forget. His people should come to appreciate that even the subtlest action prod will eventually come home to roost. Hammering home this impression is largely a matter of control. The most effective control technique I use combines a continuously updated master schedule of proposed ideas and projects in process and a simple system of secretarial followup.

If a project is significant and will cover an extended period of time, I assign a project leader responsibility for checking through on its progress and completion. He himself may have little to do with its ultimate fulfillment. But it is his job to see to it that the idea is not shelved or permitted to lag. On simpler ideas—and these often have a way of expanding into important profit contributions—my secretary, aided by her calendar and duplicate memo file, has been trained to track down all proposed ideas to their completion and to check with me where problems exist.

Thus no idea or proposal is ever lost, or permitted to fade unnoticed into oblivion. And this assurance, in my view, is of extreme importance in a company's ceaseless search for profit improvement. In the final analysis, the best way I know to move men in the direction of profit growth is through the continuing movement, interaction, and transfer of ideas.

CHAPTER FIVE

The Hat of the Marathon Runner

Shortly after the merger that formed North American Rockwell, one of the leading business monthlies sent an editor to do an article about the many and monumental tasks we faced in that vital transitional period. He interviewed me in our offices at El Segundo, California, and the articles that resulted began with a description of Chairman Al Rockwell in a great big hurry.

According to the writer, I bolted from my chair in mid-sentence when I heard the helicopter landing on the roof to whisk me away for another appointment. I rushed for the door, whirled around, and muttered: "Time—it's the scarcest thing around here."

Executive time has been called the one resource that American industry doesn't have enough of, and can't buy. Indeed, one researcher speculates that the experimental mathematical models that have been developed to aid in corporate investment decisions have failed because they have not taken into account the shortage of executive decision-time.

The original Marathon Run was just over 26 miles—the distance a Greek soldier ran from the Plains of Marathon to Athens, to tell of the great victory. *His* hat, of course, was one of those crested helmets worn by the warriors we see fighting their ageless battles on the ancient vases and amphorae (although I hope he took it off before he started jogging). But the Hat of the Marathon Runner to which I would call your attention is the laurel spray that went to the victor each year when the Marathon became the longest and most grueling of footraces. If *you* run your own race wisely and well, you will also earn the symbols of triumph.

Many presidents today run every day from early dawn to midnight—and never reach Athens. In other words, they are on a treadmill. They feel it's part of the price of their way of life. And there I will take issue with them. The corporate chief executive not only doesn't have to be on a treadmill—he had *better not* be if his company is to meet its goals. President and company must enter the gates of Athens together.

I hope I didn't sound discouraged that day when I muttered to the reporter that time was the scarcest item at North American Rockwell. Because I wasn't. To repeat, time *can* be managed so that the president can not only accomplish his tasks but can also get much more than a little fun out of life. Those safaris, those trips to the Arctic to fish for char, those regular weekends with my family (we love nothing better than just lolling about the summer place), never took anything away from business. Until recently, I even bowled regularly in the company league. These things don't diminish my business energies. They add to them, tremendously.

However, there are many times when it is necessary for me to work literally around the clock, catching ten-minute naps in cabs between appointments. Of course, there are moments when I feel utter exhaustion. Don't be deceived; every successful company leader must be something of a human dynamo of energy and drive, a person consumed by ambition for himself and for his organization.

But the great thing in running a corporation—as in running the Marathon—is *pacing*. That's how your leisure activities and your outside interests can actually contribute to your energy on the job.

HOW TO FACE A BIG DAY

March 23 began exactly as almost every day begins for me. I awoke at 6:35 A.M., lay in bed for a few minutes to organize my thoughts for the day, then dressed and had breakfast. At 8:30, the car arrived to take me to the office. My secretary, Penny Hughes, was in the car with the mail which she had just picked up. During the drive downtown, I scanned the mail, dictated some letters, and reviewed my travel schedule for the coming weeks—all routine. We arrived at the office at 8:50.

Then I talked to eight people, answered a half-dozen telephone calls, and shortly went into a meeting. By noon, several key decisions were made concerning the Rockwell-Standard merger with North American Aviation.

After lunch, I worked on strategy for one final acquisition we were making in our identity as Rockwell-Standard. It was the very important merger with the Draper Corp., the nation's largest builder of textile machinery.

In mid-afternoon, I turned to civic affairs. In my capacity as chairman of Point Park College, I issued an announcement that the historic Sherwyn Hotel would be acquired and renovated. Then it was back to business and the great event of the day. I met with the staff for 45 minutes to discuss additional details of the merger, and then two reporters came in for a one-hour news conference.

At 5 P.M., I was back at my desk, taking some 15 phone calls. Then there were a few more meetings with legal counsels and public relations people, and at 6:50 I left for home. Not a particularly long day. Hardly a Marathon Run.

The day was a very busy one, but it had pacing all the same. It also illustrated another very important factor in the management of executive time—*organization*.

On another day that I can recall, I awoke much earlier, in a hotel room in Washington. I spent the entire morning in touch-and-go conferences with government people, then climbed aboard one of our planes for New York, where a discussion about a possible merger took a sudden and unexpected turn. We had to make our move now or not at all. It was crucially important for me to fly immediately to the West Coast. Certain decisions had to be made firsthand, on the spot. I calculated the three-hour difference and decided I could just make it. In the cab out to the airport, I had a very pleasant 25-minute nap. It was the last rest I would get until late that night, I knew, because my associates and I would need almost the entire plane trip to go over our plans.

That evening, between meetings, I called home to say that as my wife may have noticed, I had not returned as scheduled—but would probably be home the next day.

Things didn't break up until the wee hours of that night. After going over every last detail, we decided to let this particular matter drop. In some ways you could say I put in that 18- or 19-hour day for nothing. But it was necessary all the same, and the key, again, was pacing and organization. That 25-minute nap in the cab kept me going.

Not too many years ago I couldn't have gone to sleep under those circumstances, with a vital deal hanging fire. Nor could I have accepted the change in schedule with equanimity. Nor could I have switched gears for the conferences and quick decisions that were required. This kind of thing takes self-control and discipline that you have no choice but to instill in yourself if you would help command a corporation in the supercharged industry of today.

And that, in any discussion of corporate Marathon Running, must be the first point to remember.

MILESTONE NUMBER 1: MENTAL CONDITIONING

Make no mistake about it. You will work, and work hard and long. E. Mandell de Windt, president of Eaton Yale & Towne, Inc., had this to say to the Cleveland Junior Chamber of Commerce:

> Energy, which unfortunately is more God-given than man-made, is an executive hallmark. Frankly I know of no successful man who has ever watched either the clock or the calendar. Success is a demanding mistress—and a man must be prepared for a total commitment of his energies.

Gerald C. Saltarelli, the blunt chairman-president of Houdaille Industries, went even further: "The men I want are those who are willing to kill themselves," he said. "I demand sacrifices . . . complete commitment and dedication." But he can make such demands because he himself sets the pace, furiously at work nine or ten hours a day, with nights and weekends spent reading voluminous reports from division heads.

Men who sight for success grow accustomed to this kind of life early. At the Harvard Business School, classes run from

8:10 A.M. until about two in the afternoon, and the students then study straight through until about midnight, customarily getting together at ten for a "can group" to discuss the next day's case histories.

To meet this kind of schedule, different men adopt different strategies. Not all the very busy men are in industry. Winston Churchill, for example, was known for his ability to take quick cat-naps at odd moments of a long day. And he spent many early hours of the morning lying in bed, propped up on pillows, while he accomplished prodigious feats of reading and dictating. In the world of show business, Arthur Godfrey saves time—about 20 to 50 minutes a day, he says—by leaping out of bed as soon as he awakens. (I prefer to rest a few moments to orient myself to the day.) Earl Wilson, the columnist, shaves in the shower. The late and great President Dwight D. Eisenhower every evening laid out his suit, shirt, tie, and other articles before retiring, so that he wouldn't lose a second in the morning—a bit of military training that he retained all his life.

But discipline like this doesn't mean you have to go around tense and tight all the time. Along with it, you can and must develop a generally relaxed attitude toward yourself and your job. It's an odd thing, but you'll find that the busier you are—if your attitude is correct—the more work you actually can take on. The president of one huge chemical company that draws its college recruiters out of the junior management ranks for temporary recruiting assignments, explains the policy this way: "We want only the real busy guys—the ones who hardly have time to go out and talk to students but manage to do it all the same. These are the men who are enthusiastic, knowledgeable, and without prejudice."

A famous business periodical, in a highly successful advertising campaign of a few years ago, said the same thing in a different way: "Only busy men," the slogan went, "have time to read the *Wall Street Journal*."

Energy, then, begets energy. But you'll have to condition yourself even more toward the habit of action. An old Buddhist saying tells us that you can study a map for years, but you're not one step closer to the city until you start walking.

Zero in on your objectives. And don't go easy on yourself, either. The British psychologist, C. A. Mace, once hit on a magnificent principle of motivation while sitting in a pub, idly watching a game of darts. Acting on his idea, he designed some laboratory experiments using a dartboard. He used two targets that were exactly the same except that one had an extra outer ring and was therefore larger in total. He set up teams to use the two targets and found that in repeated tests, the team using the smaller target scored better, even though the bullseye and the other rings were, in fact, the same size. The reason, he concluded, was that when you have a big target it's much easier to think of a bad throw as a near miss. But when you aim for a small, not so accessible target, the pressure is on you, and you perform better. You rise to the occasion.

MILESTONE NUMBER 2: PLANNING THE ROUTE

Did you ever see an ice skating race, either in person or when watching the Winter Olympics on TV? If so, you've noticed that with rare exceptions, the fastest skaters never look as though they're in a hurry. They clasp their hands behind their backs in that almost casual attitude, bend forward, and glide along the ice with those long, slow, infinitely controlled strides. The racer who frantically whips his legs and arms is very rarely a winner.

And the Marathon Runner, of course,—the real one—is also the man of superb control who lopes along for mile after mile, pacing himself, never panicking, knowing at all times exactly where he's going.

Translate this to the world of business, and you see the importance of control and organization. You don't nervously leap at your work. You calmly dip into it, producing much without any great show of activity.

Here are some of the ways it is done:

● **Knowing the route**

As I've mentioned, my own time for planning the day is usually while I'm being driven to the office. I carry along a pocketful of 4″ x 5″ cards, one for each task to be done that day. I can jot down information on each card and refer to it later in the day.

Different people work in different ways. At Michigan Millers Insurance Company, *everyone* has a "quiet hour" from 8 to 9 A.M. The entire company down to the last clerk organizes work and plans the day's activities. No outgoing telephone calls are permitted, and even conversation is held to a minimum. The system works so well for them, the company has reported, that some managers have instituted another "quiet hour" right after lunch.

No matter how you plan your schedule, make sure it is planned in some very definite fashion. My own schedule is roughed out a year in advance, then kept updated through the good offices of my very efficient secretary—and my very efficient wife. The two of them see that my business and civic appointments don't conflict, and they also work together to see how more of my time can be freed for the family.

● Avoiding detours

What's the most important part of your job as president? Well, I can tell you that it's not signing your name to sheets of paper. According to one frequently quoted authority, an executive should spend about half his time in planning ("investment time," as some call it). He should spend another 40 percent in "organization time," and about 5 percent in "payoff time" (actions having immediate benefit to the company). The last five percent, according to this expert, will unavoidably go to waste or nonproductive time.

Contrast this with the first-line supervisor, who ideally spends a full 60 percent of his time in "payoff" activities.

The point is that if you are spending too much time in nuts and bolts activities you are, in fact, "detouring" from your route as Marathon Runner. How can you keep from doing this? Take stock of your operations. If you've never done so, keep a close record of your activities for two or three weeks. Just jot down on a half-hour calendar what's going on in your office. You may be amazed at what you discover. One well-known insurance executive did this and learned, to his chagrin, that he spent most of his day "working" on the papers in his in-tray. He wasn't doing the most important parts of his job at all.

The executive, John W. May of Aetna Life & Casualty Company, made some quick adjustments. He left four hours of the day unscheduled, but then scheduled the other four hours brimming full of all the projects he had been failing to get to. And he gave each project one hour whether it was exciting or dull, fearing that otherwise he would naturally start spending too much time on the "fun" parts of the job, and not enough on the dull or even painful things, such as telling a subordinate that he is not doing well and must improve, or else.

You might ask how Mr. May found the extra time. What about the other four hours of paperwork he wasn't putting in anymore? I suspect that he condensed his efforts and also took more work home with him. But he also simply stopped doing some things—which brings us to the next point:

• Cleaning house

John May reports that he put a 30-day limit on clippings, memos, and other pieces of reading and writing. If the matter hadn't intruded itself into his schedule within 30 days, then it wasn't important enough.

You'll find that a little organization will greatly improve your own reading habits. I'm not talking about one of those speed-reading courses, although you may find that beneficial, too. But you can do a lot just by being more selective. One executive of ours, a man whose job obliges him to get through masses of reading material every week, finally confessed to me that he just couldn't keep up with it all. Together we worked out a system that has helped him. Now he:

—has his secretary pre-screen most of the material (he gave her special training for this);

—passes his eyes over an entire piece of material before starting it, so that he can pinpoint the parts he must read carefully and skim the rest;

—avoids "habit reading," by which he means going through a book from start to finish, or reading magazine articles in the order in which they appear (it's much better to skip around, according to what seems most important);

—makes copious notes, but seldom on a separate piece of paper—this executive shamelessly marks up documents, letters and books with notes that not only jog his memory if he goes back to the material, but also help to fix the information in his mind on first reading.

One other point about cleaning house: In most fields, I've found, it is possible to keep a reasonably clean desk. Many executive-time experts say the desk should have nothing on it except the project of the moment. That is carrying things too far, in my opinion. When you try to do that you end up hiding things under the blotter like a schoolboy. But a desk that is more clean than cluttered is definitely helpful. It makes for a neat mind and an orderly flow of executive decisions.

And those decisions, of course, are what it's all about. Let's discuss them now:

MILESTONE NUMBER 3: COPING WITH CROSSROADS

Ten million strong—that's how many people there are in American business who are hired basically to gather and process information to help you, the decision-maker. They include all the typists, clerks, and bookkeepers, as well as the computer programers and machine operators. Indeed, it has been pointed out that helping industry's decision-makers has become an industry in itself. The reason is that, as I've indicated earlier, executive decision-time is America's scarcest resource.

One professor of business has suggested that not too many years from now it will be quite common for every large company to have a staff officer whose sole duty it will be to advise executives on how to make the most of their hours of decision.

I know one company president, a hard-driving, fast-moving man, who took a cue from the lower ranks. He was aware of sales trainers who advise their men to think of how much each minute of their time is worth—both to themselves, in terms of their salary, and to their company, in terms of their average production. Sales journals, of course, are full of stories about men who've figured out that they make 14 cents a minute, or whatever, and by cutting coffee breaks by 20 minutes a day, can put $2.80 in their pockets. My acquaintance was aware that figures like this are at least slightly imaginary, since time in these circumstances is fairly flexible. Yet he thought it would be interesting to do the same thing with his own time, on an hourly basis.

From what he had read on the subject, he knew that just figuring out what his compensation amounted to per hour wouldn't be enough. There was also what cost experts call "opportunity dollars" for which he was responsible. So he chose an arbitrary figure and, as an experiment, began to figure out what it would "cost" him to develop certain projects he had in mind.

Without accepting his figures as anything more than examples, he began to be more aware of how the time factor should be considered in all his decisions, and in those of all the other executives in his company. For instance, an executive who is thinking of teaching his second in command to handle some recurring piece of business could estimate how much time it would take to teach him. A week? Two weeks? And how much time would the executive save by not having to do the recurring task each month? Let's say he would save about a day every month. That's only 12 days a year, so if it took more than that to teach the job, the executive would actually lose time the first year.

Furthermore, if there was a good chance that the subordinate would be promoted away from this division before long, then it would be almost certain that if the executive teaches him this particular job, he will actually *lose* time by trying to save it. So he wouldn't do it unless:

    1. the subordinate needed to know the job to perform his other duties; or,

    2. he might need to know it in his next assignment.

My friend carried this concept further and began to consider executive time as an investment—an asset to be considered whenever the company was planning new projects such as mergers, marketing expansion, new construction, etc. His financial people could tell him the expected annual return in terms of investment dollars. He added to that his own expected annual return in terms of invested man-years of executive decision-making time.

"It caused me to change my mind about some projects," he told me. "For instance, we had thought seriously about opening marketing operations in Europe for one line of products that had done quite well in the U.S. and parts of Latin America. We foresaw a reasonable payout for about 12 years, after which the products were probably going to be obsolete. It seemed like a good plan until I figured the executive time that would be involved. As our company is structured, it would have tied up key men from every function for months at a time. I decided we couldn't afford the project because it cost too much time."

Here are some ideas that should speed up your own decision-making:

● **Make each decision once**

In your decision-making, do you feel like a Marathon Runner who keeps coming back to the same crossroads? Procrastination can make anyone run in circles. When a problem comes up for your review, *decide it*. Make your decision on the spot if there's no good reason why you shouldn't. In any case, set a time limit on when you must hand in your decision to yourself. Don't let the problem simmer until it's overdone. And never put off decisions in the hope that the whole thing will just go away.

Try to handle each problem just once. You can cut your decision-making at least in half that way. It takes iron will, of course, and a profound knowledge of yourself to know the difference between procrastination and genuinely thinking it over. But these are strengths you must develop to lead a corporation.

• Program recurring decisions

One division executive of ours had set up a system of awards for his technical people. Once every quarter his managers would give him files on each of the candidates who had qualified, and he'd spend a couple of days studying them before announcing the winner. He took all kinds of things into consideration, adding his subjective evaluation to the actual record of each man.

One day he realized that his pet award program had turned into a monster. It was taking up far more of his time than could be justified by any measurement. So he had his staff engineer put it on an elaborate point system, the way it should have been in the first place. He himself took time only to review the record of the winner before extending him personal congratulations.

Almost every president must deal with certain things that come up with regularity. He can program his decisions to some extent. In other words, "Think ahead."

• Determine in advance how much time projects take

With a little effort you can get a very close estimate of how much of your executive time and others' time will be needed for such things as a new plant, the promotion of a new vice president, and so on. This is sure to help you plan a more realistic schedule.

• Improve your own decision-making process

Every man goes about it a little differently, and the basic mechanics remain slightly mysterious. But any decision is usually a matter of first gathering the facts, then designing your possible responses, and then making a choice among them. When a decision of yours goes wrong, try to see where you slipped up. Maybe you simply didn't have all the facts. Maybe you failed to realize the full implications of the response you chose. I don't believe in trying to reduce the mental processes down to a cut-and-dried stimulus response pattern. One of the reasons we executives are still at least a little better than computers is that we can taste the subtleties of human relations in our far-reaching decisions.

All the same, most of us can benefit by hard analysis of our decision-making process in an effort to improve it.

MILESTONE NUMBER 4: AID AND COMFORT

You can't do it all yourself. There are people who must run with you, though perhaps not as far or as fast. You must make use of them. Who are these people I speak of? Some of them are your own executives.

My approach to the chairmanship of a multibillion dollar company, as I told a magazine reporter at the time of the merger, was no different from my approach to running Rockwell-Standard when it was only a $700 million company. As I said at the time, management is the delegation of authority into units, and then it's up to topside to pass judgment on decisions that come up for topside consideration. As long as you're dealing with relatively large units and not too many of them—no more than nine or ten—it's not too complicated.

Most of that last passage was quoted directly by *Dun's Review*. What I meant was that I had my nine or ten units on which I depended, no matter what their size. This is the way the head of any company must operate. Delegate the authority to certain carefully selected people, and then live with the system.

Most other successful companies work more or less along these lines. John D. Phillips, the young president of R. J. Reynolds Foods, Inc., the tobacco giant's rapidly growing foods division, put the enterprise together from a patchwork of acquired producers of maple syrup, Chinese food, pudding, Mexican food, snacks, and other items. At this writing he has 11 brand managers reporting to him, and each one heads an independent profit center. Once a year the marketing plan and the budget for the coming year are agreed upon.

"Then," says Phillips, "that's it. Within their budgets the brand managers are free to do whatever they think best."

We all know of presidents who were tragically unable to make this act of faith, this act of delegation. One of them, Charles E. Zimmerman of Consultants and Designers, Inc., told his story not too long ago in *President's Forum* magazine. He had run a one-man show, with every part of his firm dependent on him— and then he had a classic coronary. Recovering, he forced himself to give up the overseeing of day-to-day operations and supervising the daily cash flow. Nor did he deal directly with lower-echelon employee problems.

He retained the "essential functions," keeping in fairly close touch with 25 major clients and watching over presidents of subsidiaries and division managers. The only people who reported directly to him under the new system, however, were the executive vice president, the treasurer, and the assistant to the president. Then Mr. Zimmerman found he had more time to take on new roles in relation with stockholders, bankers and others. He had more time for an acquisition program and to develop the management team.

"I still see the same amount of papers on my desk," he said. "But the difference is that the papers I now see are more important."

There is, of course, another important group of people the wise executive depends upon. These are his outside consultants. These people, carefully chosen, can lengthen your shadow.

Specifically, various kinds of consultants can help you open up new programs by doing market surveys, employee-attitude surveys, plant and equipment studies, diversification studies, and more. Others can recruit executives or train lower ranking personnel. Still other kinds of consultants can help solve problems such as high turnover, drastic product mix, or declining sales. And they can all, as I indicated earlier, help you plan for the future.

It's not only people, however, who can aid you in your long-distance run. You should also have the benefit of the very best equipment the company can possibly afford, including computers. Not long ago computers were considered the province, or perhaps the plaything, of only the giant corporations. That is definitely not the case today. According to a recent survey by the Research Institute of America, any company with at least 200 employees and sales of $7 million that does not have access to a computer, either through leasing the equipment or hiring the time, is in a clear minority in American industry today. Users outnumbered non-users in all types of businesses. Even more significantly, 16 percent of the non-users planned to acquire EDP facilities within a year, and 58 percent of these non-users already had an EDP-educated member of the top management team. The study concluded: "Any smaller business that isn't using a computer—its own or an outside service center—should have a good reason why not."

Your company will probably fall badly behind unless you keep up with these new developments. A word of caution, however: Computers *do not* save top management time. They increase the *quality* of your decisions and your planning, but they don't do it for you.

Here is a piece of equipment, however, that *does* save executive time: an airplane. Far from being a useless extravagance or a sop to executive ego, as some have claimed, the company airplane is virtually indispensable to the executive who must visit installations in cities not well served by the major airlines. Believe me, there are hundreds of such cities in the U.S. One executive in Shreveport, Louisiana, finds it necessary to make personal inspections fairly often in Tulsa, Fort Worth, and Amarillo. In the past he tried to do it by commercial airline and would literally waste days per trip. The choice seemed to be either giving up the trips or investing in a company plane. He chose the latter.

"One of these days we'll all be talking to each other on TV consoles," he says. "But I think I'll still want to see people in person. That's the only way to catch the nuances in voice tone and facial expression that tell you how business is *really* going. There's no substitute for eyeball-to-eyeball contact."

MILESTONE NUMBER 5: SAVING YOUR WIND

The long-distance runner doesn't sprint all the way, nor does he run at the same speed throughout the race. He must, I repeat, pace himself. This is a real science, a matter of self-control.

I would venture that the major obstacles to sensible pacing on the part of a business executive can be summarized in one word:

worry. That is what keeps you from refreshing yourself with a good night's sleep. That is what keeps you from being able to dismiss your concerns for a quick nap on your office sofa or in a cab, in the middle of a marathon day. That is what makes every task seem harder or more complex than it really is, and what makes you fearful of an important decision that can be put off no longer.

In a few moments' time or even in an entire book, I can hardly tell you how to get rid of civilized man's most universal complaint. But I will tell you this—you must control your worries or they will control you.

Once, years ago, when an important merger had fallen through, with what seemed to be serious consequences for our company, an associate asked me how I could take the matter so calmly. I told him, as simply as I could, that I had made a series of decisions on how to proceed, on the basis of the best information I could gather. It now appeared that the plan was the wrong one, but I had done the very best I could and that was that. Rather than bemoaning past mistakes or ill luck, the thing to do now was to start setting into motion the contingency plan that we had developed earlier for just such an emergency.

It is, of course, a temperamental thing—an attitude that you must develop. Your wife can help you. I know that it helps me to talk things out with Constance at the end of a long and difficult day. She's something of a Marathon Runner herself, with her hospital and charitable work, her post as director of the Pittsburgh Civic Light Opera Guild, and all her other activities. And she understands both the business and social worlds as few women do.

Another company president I know depends on his wife's advice even more. She told my wife recently that her husband believes she has a genius for solving knotty "people problems" in the executive suite. What he does is pace the living room, asking her questions and then dourly supplying the answers himself. In a half-hour or so he has the problem all worked out in his mind. Then he smiles and kisses her and says: "You've done it again."

"And half the time," his wife privately confesses, "I'm not even sure what he's talking about."

You'll also find it helpful, I believe, if you try to enlarge your life beyond the boundaries of business. My wife and I have treasured the stimulating friendships we have cultivated with people in such fields as the arts, education, and government. We a'so enjoy our vacations to the very fullest, and I've mentioned we have found that quite often it is possible to combine business and pleasure on, say, a trip to Europe. You don't have to shut out business from your mind for three weeks in order to enjoy a change of pace and a change of scene. With the communications networks that exist today, an executive can literally have the best of both worlds for at least a short time.

The trend, incidentally, is definitely this way. The Chicago Association of Commerce and Industry reports that among its top-management members, 51 percent now take off a month or more during the year, and 28 percent now split their time off between summer and winter vacations. Most take off more or less when they choose, not trying to coincide their absences with a plant shutdown or the like. All these trends were much more pronounced than just a few years ago, the Chicago group says.

Most executives spend their vacations sightseeing, and there is also emphasis among these men on participation, not on spectator sports.

Perhaps the most revealing statistic, however, was that 27 percent of the companies surveyed make vacations mandatory for their executives. In other words, the boss has no choice but to get away from the desk and renew his energies.

MILESTONE NUMBER 6: TAKING SHORTCUTS

Unlike the real athlete, the Marathon Runner in business need not keep to the beaten path. If he sees a shortcut through a mountain pass, he can and probably should take it. The problem, of course, is to see it in the first place.

In some ways the executive operates like the salesman who keeps his eyes and ears open as he drives through his territory between calls. A good salesman looks for new construction and business activity that might hold out the promise of new customers. He searches for evidence of local affairs such as politics or civic programs that might influence the character of each community. The executive, too, must never stop asking himself what the things he is seeing might mean to his business.

One foods executive I know sampled a native vegetable in a

Central American country and later imported it for use in his line of prepared foods. Again, oil firms noticed the success of self-service stations in Europe, and introduced them in parts of this country. One of my favorite examples of all, though, in this matter of keeping your eyes open, involves those gladiators of the car rental industry, Hertz and Avis.

As everyone knows, Avis has used a series of clever, often humorous advertisements that have won a number of awards and have also produced solid marketing results. One Avis print ad showed a picture of the Kremlin with a headline: "There is no Avis office in Moscow. But we're working on it."

The Hertz management saw the ad, too, and it gave them an idea. They opened negotiations in Russia and a few years later had an agreement with Intourist, the Soviet travel organization, to franchise Hertz operations in some 20 Russian cities and resort towns. The name will be different since there is no "H" in the Russian alphabet, but the yellow-and-black signs will be the same, and eventually the Soviet counter girls will wear uniforms like those in this country.

Avis sighted the pass. But Hertz took the shortcut. Inspiration is of little value unless you act on it. And that, I would suggest, is another lesson from the Marathon Runner.

MILESTONE NUMBER 7: NEVER GET OUT OF CONDITION

Being a Marathon Runner begin and ends with this rule. Part of it is physical. To lead your company you must have moderate habits of eating and drinking. You must get enough rest. You must keep your physical resources in sound working order.

But the part that trips up many a would-be corporate runner is the mental conditioning that I mentioned at the beginning. Just in case I haven't made it clear, let me say again that your own domestic tranquility is easily the most important contributor to this mental conditioning. A wife who understands what it is to be a president's wife, and the demands of the "job," is simply the greatest treasure the ambitious man can have.

But let's not be solemn about it. There's a little gamesmanship, too, in this matter of dividing your life so that no area of it is slighted, and so that you don't feel under constant pressure. The other day Constance was telling me about the devotion of the husband of a friend of hers. This woman, it seems, loves amateur theatricals and had been rehearsing a new play for weeks. When it opened, her husband, a senior executive, was supposed to be on an important business trip to London. But he cancelled the trip and stayed home to toast her performance. Here, if ever, was real devotion.

I must have had a rather amused look on my face, because Constance asked me what I was thinking about.

"Well, I have an idea the trip wasn't as important as he played it up to be," I said, chuckling. "My guess is he's a better actor than she is. But what does it matter as long as she loves it?"

Then it was my wife's turn to laugh. "How good an actor are you, Al?" she asked. "Did you really enjoy my animal costume party last summer, after the safari, as much as you said you did?"

"Can't imagine *what* you're talking about," I responded, hoping to drop the subject.

CHAPTER SIX

The Hat of the Lord Chief Justice

This one, of course, isn't exactly a hat. It's a periwig. And I hope it doesn't symbolize stodginess to you, or rigid attitudes of thought. It is true that a judge must operate within the firm framework of the law, but within that framework his responsibility calls for him to be nothing less than a philosopher. His mind must be quiet, reflective, thoughtful, and open.

As a chief executive, you must be the daily judge of the performance of hundreds of people, many of whom you have never met. You must have a very good idea of how well or how poorly everyone in the company is doing. No, you can't say offhand whether the machine shop foreman in East St. Louis got to work on time today. But through the mass of information that flows in, you do know whether that individual and others like him are doing a generally good job.

But evaluation starts, of course, with those near the bench —your key executives with whom you have daily contact.

Or does it? Perhaps evaluation starts somewhere else. In *Pelleas and Melisande,* Maeterlinck has an anguished old man cry out: "I have never for one instant seen clearly within myself; how then would you have me judge the deeds of others?" Nor can you, as Lord Chief Justice of your company, appraise those under you unless you have a very clear idea of the conflicts and motivations that go on underneath your own wig. In my opinion, the two appraisals—of yourself and your people—go hand in hand. But more of that later.

SYSTEMATIC EVALUATION—WHY SO URGENT?

Systematic evaluation permits you to move confidently towards your objectives with the expectation of achievement. Using hit or miss evaluation, you move forward blindly, if at all. Here is a sampling of benefits achieved at North American Rockwell which I hold in large measure attributable to our performance-appraisal strategies.

1. The pinpointing of individual strengths and weaknesses at all levels of performance.
2. A more meaningful meeting of minds.
3. The setting of realistic, attainable goals.
4. Clarification of the means of attaining objectives.
5. Elimination of unessential tasks.
6. Time saved through the avoidance of error and misunderstanding.
7. The pooling and emulation of successful techniques.
8. Problems placed in fresh perspective.
9. Establishment of action and goal-setting priorities.
10. Conversion of good intentions into profit-motivated action.
11. The sorting of leaders from leaners, problem solvers from postponement specialists.
12. Maximum use of human resources; application of career-building techniques.
13. Guidance in assigning key projects and structuring the organization.

PART I—REVIEWING YOUR PEOPLE

With an eye on tomorrow

An article in *Business Week* was headed, HELP WANTED —ALMOST EVERYWHERE. A sub-head might well have read, *In the Executive Suite Especially.*

Never in my memory has competition been keener for managers of proven ability. A friend in the tool machine business told me recently:

> I can remember the day when finding markets for our products was the number one problem of our company. Have times changed! Today markets are number two. First on the list is finding good men to sell our products, manage our divisions, and help run our company.

I think you will find this story repeated in every industry from steamships to hot dogs. As a matter of fact, Nathan's Famous, Inc., the nation's best known maker of hot dogs, has just invested heavily to recruit a top management team for its new franchise division. And it wasn't easy.

Obviously, the shrinking market for executive talent makes it doubly essential to grow your own leaders successfully. The trick is to smoke out the climbers in your organization and apply just the right mix of guidance and motivation to enable their personal aspirations to dovetail with your goals and expectations. Identifying the abilities, in my experience, is the easy part of this job. What is often more difficult is measuring the calibre of the man to determine that he is not only able, but also willing, to make maximum use of his talents.

Call it drive, call it thrust, call it ambition—his will to succeed is not always easy to pin down. In the end, as author-consultant Peter Drucker puts it, "Everything degenerates into work."

How hard is your emerging young leader willing to work? Not in terms of hours, necessarily; these will be irregular and unpredictable at times, but in the main, most progressive corporations discourage exhaustively long hours and recognize the value of relaxation. The key questions are these: What is your climber climbing toward? *How much of himself is he willing to invest to get what he wants?*

I can recall the case of a young man within our own organization. His talents were apparent to all. But how badly did he want to move to a high executive post? I decided to find out. Presenting a difficult project for his consideration, I asked him to mull it over and come back to me with his thoughts on the subject.

He appeared the following morning with ten typewritten sheets filled with ideas. I mentally calculated his trip to the library and several hours of work until at least three or four in the morning. I had the answer I sought.

The project involved some traveling. "How soon can you fly to Atlanta?" I asked. "I can go home and pack and be ready in an hour." I laughed and suggested he make it the following day. "I think you can use a good night's sleep."

The point is this. Leadership implies dedication. Some executives expect this from every manager and supervisor. And they're right, to a degree. But being completely realistic, the amount of dedication you are entitled to expect depends pretty much on the value of the prize. A top management job, of course, demands total commitment and total dedication.

By this I mean willingness—*not a reluctant willingness, but a genuine desire*—to put up with the pressures, irregular hours, globe hopping, family life disruption, intensive study and concentration that the executive job demands. It means trading X hours of contract bridge, golf, TV viewing or whatever outside activities appeal to you, in order to move your company's objectives along with them.

I don't believe that total dedication is the obligation of every employee. But the manager who wishes to move up must realize that he will climb only as far as his degree of dedication permits him to climb. It is a choice that we all have to make. There is an increasingly high toll in dedication as the atmosphere rarefies. And it is a key task, in appraising your people, to find out precisely how large a price they are willing to pay.

If your man aspires to a vice presidency, for example, would he be willing to accept two years of overseas service if this were a stepping stone to the job? What if achieving this goal meant relocating from a suburban to an urban environment or vice versa? How does his wife feel about his objectives? Does she share his ambition? Or are his personal goals in conflict with her real desires? It can make a world of difference. When the aspirations of husband and wife are compatible, they will work and sacrifice for them as a team, and gain excitement and satisfaction through the mutual effort. If they are in conflict, it can tear a family apart. This is bad for the wife, for the executive, for the family, and ultimately for the company. It's the kind of thing you should learn about in advance, before grooming your key people for responsible leadership posts.

Can he walk alone?

The executive with leadership potential possesses four main characteristics, according to Professor Eli Ginzberg of Columbia University: "strong personal goals—he knows where he wants to go; abundant physical and emotional energy; a willingness to take risks—to be different, to take the consequences for decisions, good and bad; and political skill—the ability to influence and manage people."

What's more, I find, the leader of men has initiative to spare. He tackles problems with zest, but his main focus is on solutions. To illustrate, in one company a central purchasing department bought parts and supplies for three divisions. Each division was headed by a plant manager who reported to the vice president of manufacturing. One day, one of the plant managers appeared in the vice president's office looking especially harassed. He reported a rash of production problems and equipment failures. Critical measures were called for to get to the root of the trouble and steer the operation back on course.

Contacting another plant manager, the vice president learned he was experiencing the same kind of difficulty. "But I think I've got it tracked down," manager number two said. As it turned out, he had found that the failures and breakdowns had started about the same time as an austerity program launched by the purchasing department. They were going overboard in an effort to pare costs. Suppliers, being pushed too hard, had been forced to cut corners.

Important to note is the difference between the two plant managers. One came to the boss with a problem; the other with a solution. One needed a superior to hold his hand; the other walked alone.

Not all executives have the stuff it takes to walk alone. I think it is a vital part of the appraisal process to separate the walkers from the toddlers, to shore up or compensate for weaknesses when they appear.

Another case in point comes to mind. Here a technically trained middle manager possessed a unique talent for selling programs and ideas. On the surface it appeared that this man would go far in the company. Closer analysis, however, pointed up an important weakness. He could *sell* ideas, but rarely *had* one. He had no heart for the tough lonely chore of digging into complex problems and coming up with alternative solutions. Actually, he had missed his calling. He was better equipped for sales than engineering.

When his boss leveled with him, the man was delighted. Within the week he was transferred to sales, and a talented engineer was assigned to back up his persuasive skills with technical depth. The engineer, ill at ease with people, was a perfect counterpart for the other. The pair worked as an effective selling team. The strengths of one man compensated for the weaknesses of the other, an essential objective of the appraisal program.

It is a thought to keep in mind. Where a man cannot walk alone, it is sometimes excellent strategy to provide a companion to walk beside him.

Reinforce your judgment

The English cleric Charles Mildmay once said, "Reasoning against a prejudice is like fighting against a shadow; it exhausts the reasoner without visibly affecting the prejudice."

I have seen this borne out in business again and again. An executive is no more objective in his appraisal of subordinates than his prejudices permit him to be. Most executives I know honestly try to shake off their prejudices. Some succeed in hiding them, even from their own eyes. Others stubbornly cling to them. But it is the rare executive who is totally devoid of prejudices. Which only proves that executives, just like astronauts, ball players and bank tellers, are merely human.

Most prejudices you come into contact with are subtle and elusive. They run the gamut from bias about manner, appearance, and cultural level to intolerance regarding the military, politicians, women in general and blondes in particular—not to mention the more obvious and odious prejudices linked to race and religion.

I know one executive who is partial to tall men. Not one manager on his staff is under six feet in height. The executive is aware of this bias—he calls it a quirk—but cannot explain it. I have seen a gifted director of sales who could talk a disciple of Mao into singing the "Star Spangled Banner." Yet he cannot tolerate his assistant because the man holds a doctorate degree in philosophy.

My point is simply this: However objective you believe your appraisal to be, chances are it is colored in some measure at least by some prejudices, conscious or hidden. I think it is extremely difficult for most people to cast aside intolerance completely and take on what Edmund Burke called "the cold neutrality of an impartial judge." I find it a good idea to reinforce my own judgment regarding any man's abilities by soliciting the judgment of others.

A highly successful chief executive officer told me recently: "In appraising my key people, I try to back my own opinion with the *independent* ratings of at least two others in a superior position to the person being rated. If the ratings match, there is no problem. If they are in some disparity, I give them further consideration. When items are in sharp disagreement, I know that a depth probe is in order."

And insist that those ratings be specific. Vague generalization about a man's abilities or potential can be misleading, a prime burial ground for conscious or sub-conscious prejudices. For example, if the independent rater feels the subject does not get along well with his associates, get him to illustrate cases to prove his point. If he says the subject contributes good ideas, have him spell out examples. I can recall one situation where a manager was rated "highly creative" by two indirect superiors, but not by his boss. As it turned out, the creativeness was secondhand. The manager had taken to spouting in a proprietary manner ideas originally proposed by other people.

In my view, accurate appraisal is vitally important to the growth and continued well-being of any organization—so much so that it cannot be left to chance or to the hazards of misinterpretation.

Put key men to the test

As many high level executives have learned, a manager is in a kind of running contest with the talented young climbers on his staff. It is a matter of discovering a man's potential and cashing in on it before he discovers it for himself and comes to the conclusion that he can move faster elsewhere.

In my little Blue Book of Business Mistakes, one stands out in particularly sharp relief. And a name I see often in the business press these days calls it constantly to mind. The individual in question once worked for me as a young engineer. His talent was apparently larger than I perceived at the time. I failed to properly recognize his ability or give him the elbow room he needed to exercise his initiative, an error I have been trying diligently not to repeat. In any case, the man up and left one day. He is now running an important division of a fast-growing company, and in no small measure he is responsible for its growth. It does not give me the best of feelings when, in retrospect, I consider that it is one of our divisions he might be running, and my own company's growth that he might be adding to.

There is a great need, I think, and one that many otherwise capable executives sometimes overlook, constantly to put promising subordinates to the test. You cannot learn too early, experience shows, about the leadership potential your people possess. And obtaining this knowledge is rarely a passive procedure.

Often, when I have a challenging project on tap, I throw it up for grabs. Getting people to volunteer for a task, I find, is often more effective than routinely assigning it. For one thing, it is a way of determining the preferences of your key people. For another, it gives the climber an opportunity to stretch his own capacities.

Within the scope of their abilities and limitations, of course, I am a strong believer in testing my key people to the hilt. And the only truly effective place to test them is on the job itself. Often, I think, there is too high a dependence on classroom or training results. I have seen too many instances of brilliant scholars converted into floundering managers.

As Dr. Peter Drucker says, "Until a man has actually been under fire, an old military proverb says, there is no way of predicting whether he will make a soldier or not. Unless a man has been in the spot where he had to make the decisions and take responsibility for them, he has not been tested. He usually has not even been trained."

Nathaniel Stewart, writing for *Nation's Business*, echoes Drucker's sentiments: "The comer can best be identified by his behavior under firing line conditions. Some of these indications stand out more visibly than others. Watch out for them. The comer shows early that he is able to handle his own duties— plus. It is the plus dimension which sets a rising leader apart from the ordinary supervisor."

The subordinate who shows early signs of talent bears especially close watching. Observation, I have found, is the prime key to resultful appraisal. Watch your man without giving him the impression you are breathing down his back. Test him by letting out the line gently but persistently. See how far he will go on his own. If he appears to be proceeding too gingerly, bolster his confidence by demonstrating your faith in his ability —even if it means risking an error or two along the way. As Plutarch said, "To make no mistakes is not in the power of man, but from their errors and mistakes the wise and good learn wisdom for the future."

Make appraisal a joint undertaking

An attitude-evaluation expert recently completed a study for a large Government agency. In one department, where performance was subpar, he interviewed a top manager regarding his chief assistant's work. Then, independently, he interviewed the assistant on the same subject. The two interviews were at complete variance.

The boss listed one set of objectives for the subordinates; the assistant listed another. Some goals on the boss's list did not appear on the assistant's and vice versa. Priorities were inconsistent. The assistant assessed himself as possessing certain abilities the boss did not recognize. The boss cited weaknesses which, as far as the assistant was concerned, were new. Is it any wonder the two men were incompatible and the operation stymied?

For appraisal to be meaningful, it must be conducted along a two-way street. A continuing dialogue between the appraiser and the appraised will help spot obstacles and de-fog the atmosphere. Without such feedback, projects bog down. Unaired gripes fester into program-blocking bitterness. A periodic comparison of actual results against expected results, on the other hand, helps to keep objectives on target. It provides assurance that the implementation of your plans is in line with your intentions. And it helps you pinpoint imperfections in your goals, standards, and deadlines, and make realistic adjustments before the imperfections deteriorate into goal-defeating roadblocks.

How important is mutual agreement? Suggests Professor Earl Brooks of Cornell University:

> For each of your immediate subordinates write out a statement of conditions which should exist six months from now when the subordinate's responsibilities are carried out to your satisfaction. Then ask each subordinate to write out, independently of your appraisal, what he thinks par will be for his job in the way of accomplishment six months from now. Compare the statements. If there is 75 percent agreement on important factors, the understanding and expectations between superior and subordinate are probably better than those of your average competitor.

As a bank director friend told me recently, "The trouble with two-way discussion is that to some executives it means the boss lecturing, the subordinate listening."

This confirms my own experience. For dialogue to be helpful, the value of the dialogue itself must first be made evident. It should be an exchange experience, not a soliloquy or diatribe. The discussion should be interesting and beneficial. It should analyze problems, review progress, and establish mutually acceptable goals for the period ahead. It should be an experience that both parties look forward to with anticipation and enjoyment.

OPERATION PROBE

How can you distinguish the subordinate who is leadership material from the man who is destined to settle into an inconspicuous middle slot and stay there the rest of his life? Here are some pertinent questions that may prove helpful:

1. Is he skillful at sorting the trivial from the important, delegating lesser tasks, and setting priorities realistically?
2. Is he unwilling to tolerate sloppiness or compromise on standards?
3. Is he intelligently responsive to criticism?
4. Does he inspire excellence in others and motivate people to rally to his causes?

5. Does he remain strong under pressure, resolute when the going is rough?
6. Does he genuinely enjoy his job?
7. Is he curious about activities outside his immediate realm?
8. Do new ideas excite him; is he receptive to the ideas of others; does he create ideas of his own; does he go all out to sell ideas he believes in?
9. Does he get along easily and naturally with people on all levels?
10. Does he plan and organize his work effectively, anticipate obstacles well in advance?
11. Does he seek help from others when he needs it?
12. Does he possess the resiliency needed to bounce back from setbacks?
13. Does he express himself clearly and show a willingness to listen to the views of others?
14. Is he receptive to the views of others, even when they are contrary to his own views?
15. Does he respect, credit, and reward the outstanding performance of his subordinates?

PART II—REVIEWING YOURSELF

Level with yourself

William Wordsworth called self-inspection the best cure for self-esteem. But for most executives, objective self-appraisal takes an ample dose of self-discipline. The key role of ego drive in achieving executive success has been too well covered by the management press for me to labor it here. Still, it does take on a special significance for the manager who is seriously interested in identifying his weaknesses and shoring them up. Such an individual finds himself faced with the delicate task of balancing his healthy egoism against a compelling desire for self-improvement.

It's not easy. As a wit points out, "There are two kinds of egotists: those who admit it, and the rest of us." But another student of business observes on a more sober note: "When a man is really important, the worst adviser he can have is a flatterer."

One fact of high executive life is certain. If flattery is your dish, you can get all you want. For one thing, the average executive *is* much above average in intelligence and capability. Moreover, however humble you may strive to be, you are well aware of your superiority, and you would be less than human if it did not make you just a little smug on occasion.

Adding fuel to the boss's smugness is the respect—sometimes bordering on reverence—of his subordinates. The executive who thinks he's "the greatest" usually finds ample support for his conviction. Particularly if he lets his people know that such support meets with his approval.

The problem then is to retain the ego drive you need to lead men and make crucial decisions, and at the same time, to assess your performance in an honest and meaningful way. The trick, in my experience, is to keep each of your two identities in its proper perspective. First there is the "you" you would like to be. That's the one that gets flattery. Then there is the real "you," the executive with many powerful strengths, but with a sprinkling of weaknesses mixed in. Recognizing the weaknesses that exist is an essential ingredient of successful self-appraisal. From what I have seen, the executive who believes himself totally lacking in weaknesses is usually the weakest of all.

One might also argue that no executive would deliberately take an action that he knows to be weak. And there you have the hub of the problem. To pinpoint your weaknesses and take steps to correct them, you are going to need help. And the way to get help is to slap down subservience on the one hand, and gain skill in identifying objectivity on the other.

Just as you will need backup evidence in your support appraisals of subordinates, so you will need backup evidence in assessing your own abilities. But in this case it will be less easy to come by. You cannot always tell a subordinate: "Skip the flattery, Bill. Tell me what you really think." You may be able to say this to a close associate at times, but rarely to a lower echelon employee.

Still, there are ways of getting around the dilemma. For one thing, you are as good as your program and ideas. Agreement with what you do constitutes an endorsement of your performance. Disagreement, if you take positive steps to discourage blind endorsement, can serve as a powerful appraisal tool. The idea is to get the whys and wherefores and to clamp down on the "yes men" in your organization. If a subordinate claims that his views coincide with yours, find out why. Where possible, explore his thinking before you reveal your own decision. Require him to come up with specific arguments to either support or refute your thinking. And mold your heroes of the men who show enough courage to intelligently oppose the boss.

Place a premium on courage

It is not always easy to listen to the sound of other drummers when the one you want to hear beats loudly in your ears.

Several months ago, a company I know developed an exciting new product line. The marketing people boiled over with enthusiasm. The president, a strongly growth-oriented executive, was swept along by the tide of this fervor. He painted a glowing picture of the potential to the financial vice president, an astute executive whose views always had been carefully weighed by the president in formulating his own decisions. Privately, the man was not so sure the product line was ready for market. He had heard rumblings and grumblings from Manufacturing and Engineering regarding problems they were running into. But, reluctant to buck such formidable opposition as Marketing and the chief executive, he said nothing. The line was introduced to the market place.

As it turned out, the introduction was premature. The technical and production segments were unable to keep pace with Marketing's go-go enthusiasm. Not all items were fully developed. Not all bugs were completely eradicated. Almost from the first day, customer complaints started pouring in. The company's excellent quality image was seriously undermined.

The president, crestfallen, called in a consultant to determine why and how the blunder had been made. His findings, emerging mainly from a series of soul-searching interviews, were blunt and revealing. The financial executive, manufacturing and engineering managers, and others bared their true feelings which in the main had been squelched by the Marketing-president combine.

"The devil's advocates were never given a chance to air their views," the consultant said simply.

As a result of the consulting experience, meaningful changes were made. The promotion and compensation machinery was altered so that automatic increases and advancement for top and middle management were discontinued. Performance was more

closely and systematically appraised, with an eye on specific contributions. An "executive sorting" system was installed whereby
the status quo advocates and bandwagon hoppers, comfortably
ensconced in their ruts, were distinguished from the company's
courageous climbers.

The president learned, in seeking counsel, to call on the climbers and sidestep the "yes men." He also learned to cloak his own
opinions so as to get the free and unbiased independent judgment of others. "I found out too," he told me recently, "that if
you want the truth, you have to convince people of your willingness to accept it."

Single out your lesser strengths

From what I have seen, successful top executives in general
have considerable vision and widespread experience. On the
whole they are intelligent people, widely read, intellectually curious. Yet there are but few men who, like Winston Churchill,
possess the brand of genius which communicates itself to everything they touch. Though generalists in the main, most executives have talents that center strongly about a specific area of
administration—law, finance, marketing, engineering—depending
on their business background and training.

My point is this. Though top executive responsibilities cover
a wide scope of company activities, traditionally the high level
manager possesses maximum strength and confidence in some
areas, a measure of uncertainty in others. The executive with a
heavy technical background, for example, may find himself a
trifle testy when called upon to make judgments in accounting
or marketing areas. The executive who comes up via the marketing route may feel even more uncomfortable in dealing with
manufacturing requirements.

Writing for *Nation's Business*, Research Institute of America
editor Auren Uris asks: "Are you a four-way expert?" He divides
the executive's people. The paperwork aspect, according to the
author, requires the accountant's keen eye for detail. Planning
calls for imagination and creativity. To excel procedurally, one
needs financial talents and ability to "think technical." Handling
people skillfully requires a sensitivity to individual feelings and
attitudes, the ability to "think human."

As Uris points out, few of us are flexible enough to master all of these diverse qualities. The ideal in self-appraisal is to recognize our greater strengths, our lesser strengths, our outright weaknesses for what they are.

Once these are accurately defined and solidly ingrained, we can concentrate on applying weaknesses and strengths to the improvement of our personal productivity. An executive can ask: Am I cashing in on my financial acumen to the maximum? Is my superficial understanding of chemical processing hindering my performance in any way? Should I devote more effort to studying certain aspects of the operation? Should I be shoring up a specific weakness, or should I compensate for it by delegating the responsibility?

The idea, of course, is to relate such questions to your own operation. A byproduct of self-appraisal that I find particularly fruitful is the pinpointing of areas where weaknesses block or delay profit objectives. Once the situation has been spotlighted, remedying the problem becomes merely a matter of course.

Develop reliable sources of objectivity

A close friend of mine is senior vice president in a large service organization which shall remain unnamed. He recently came to me with a problem that was distressing him. He was convinced that his boss, the president, through a stubborn refusal to modernize a product line, was running a key division into the ground. After hearing the circumstances involved, I was inclined to agree.

"He's absolutely adamant," my friend said. "I can't think of any way to get him to change his course without putting my own neck in jeopardy."

Thinking realistically, it is easy to suggest to people that they exercise courage and, where necessary, even martyr themselves in defense of their convictions. In practice, it doesn't work this way. A man who works hard all his life does not easily risk losing what he has gained in the name of principle or anything else. Not if the likelihood of loss seems real and probable.

In this case, discussion led to a practical solution. My friend was able to recruit a key customer to his cause. The customer, a man of considerable stature and influence, succeeded in virtually browbeating the president into seeing the light. The dual objective of getting the message through and, at the same time, keeping my friend off the hook, was accomplished.

Not every such situation turns out as happily. Not always does a skidding executive have an associate with sufficient foresight and determination to steer him back on course. And in spite of your best efforts, not always can you find people within your own organization who are inclined—or indeed qualified—to offer their honest opinion in every area of performance.

In my experience, shooting for free expression, encouraging subordinates to level with the boss, rewarding courage and honesty, are worth every drop of energy you can put into the effort. But it is not always the ultimate answer. Sometimes I find it is helpful to go a step further to assure objective assessment of complex problems and difficult decisions—and the use of a good consultant who can serve as combination sounding board and executive conscience. One president I know leans heavily for such counsel on the now retired chairman who was his former mentor.

Besides our consultants, I have a mentor of my own, my father, Colonel Rockwell, whom I hold to be one of the most astute businessmen of this century. In any case, my point is that the harder you search for total objectivity in your self-appraisal effort, the more certainly will your goal-defeating weaknesses be brought to the operating table for surgery.

Operation probe

What key signs should you look for in examining your personal performance with an eye on self-improvement? Here is a sampling of provocative questions to get you started. Others of your own choosing and applicable to your own operation will undoubtedly come to mind as you consider this list.

1. If you were one of your subordinates, would you select yourself as your superior?
2. Can you name specific contributions you've made in the past six months to contribute to your company's profit growth?
3. Do you jointly agree upon goals with your people, and keep achievement expectations fair and reasonable with the limitations of your subordinates in mind?
4. Are your people convinced that performance alone is your barometer for awarding recognition, advancement, and increased compensation?

5. Do your people and you share the same definitions of their goals, responsibilities, and limits of authority?
6. Are you careful to keep every promise you make?
7. Do you have a program of *tangible* recognition—not lip service—for innovation within your group?
8. Do you segregate essential from nonessential tasks, and properly delegate the non-essentials to subordinates?
9. Do you ever review your progress periodically to ensure that your good intentions are being converted into profit action?
10. Are your people genuinely convinced that you are personally concerned about their well-being?
11. How successfully do you transfer your own enthusiasm regarding projects, programs, and ideas to other people?
12. Are your people ever reluctant to present an idea to you because they are fearful of the consequences if proven wrong?
13. Do you take positive steps to upgrade your speaking, writing, and *listening* skills?
14. Do you make a strong effort to tie the personal career objectives of your people to the profit objectives of the company?
15. Are you thoroughly convinced that you explore and exploit the talents of your people to the maximum?

If you can come up with ten or more "yes" answers, you've earned your position in the high court. Wear your wig in good health!

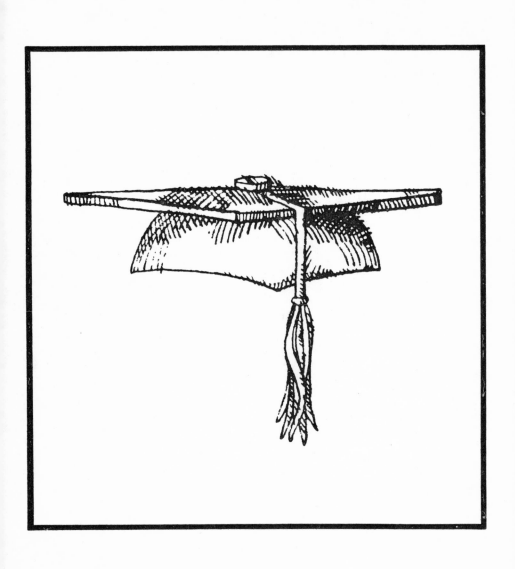

CHAPTER SEVEN

The Hat of the Student

In a way, this headgear is misleading. That well-loved flat cap with its tossing fringe implies graduation. And it is my view that the truly successful chief executive *never* graduates. In other words, he never stops learning. And neither do his subordinates. We are all of us eternal undergraduates on the great campus of industrial society.

Unfortunately, this campus, like the academic ones, has its share of disorders and even an occasional riot. And all too many of these conflicts are caused by the poor quality of the instruction.

American business spends from $17 billion to $35 billion per year to train and retrain its people, depending on which expert estimate you like best. Whatever figure you settle for, you can be certain your company's training investment is a substantial slice of the corporate budget. And the profit-yielding effectiveness of the program could very well spell the difference between failure and success in your organization. Strategies and techniques used to impart knowledge to employees at all levels from president on down must be of major concern to the corporate executive.

As one chief executive remarked recently: "The way I read it, any person holding a job of importance in tomorrow's business world will find it necessary to upgrade his knowledge on a regular and continuing basis."

My personal experience bears out this contention. I have found that the higher a manager ranks in the corporate echelon, the more significant the quality of his training becomes. I also regret to report that in too many companies I have seen top ranking managers become too bogged down with everyday affairs to adequately broaden and develop their own management skills. Not that the everyday function is not a learning process in itself. It is perhaps one of the most instructive aspects of all. But there also must be planned and deliberate self-improvement of a different nature—the kind that necessitates getting away from the daily routine to stand back and view your business and your life from a broader and deeper perspective.

This kind of self-improvement isn't easy. It takes much persistence and self-discipline. But it is a goal we at North American Rockwell strive for constantly and diligently.

BUILD THE MAN AS WELL AS THE MANAGER

In my view, the manager who makes it to the top in the seventies and eighties will not be a super-specialist; he will not be the manager with exposure to and expertise in one limited area of the business, and information gaps in other areas that are like great empty barns with the wind whistling through them. He will be a cultured and well-rounded individual.

Knowledge enriches knowledge, and the more the variety, the greater the enrichment. A financial manager, for example, may hammer away endlessly at the financial aspects of the business. Assuming he is endowed with ample intelligence and that the necessary specialized training is provided, he may become a so-called financial wizard in time. But wizard or not, he will be limited both as a manager and as a person if his education is confined to financial aspects exclusively. He will be limited in working with and dealing with people. He will be limited in relating financial considerations to other aspects of the business such as marketing, research, and manufacturing. He will be limited in projecting the desired corporate image. He will be limited in generating the warmth and rapport that are so essential to the development of trust relationships at high levels and the consummation of important business deals.

That is not to say no important place in business will exist for the specialized manager. He will always be needed. But the top man of the future, in my view, will be the specialist plus. His abilities will grow like a mushroom, not like a bean sprout.

The broadening process I have in mind will not just happen. It can occur only by design. A manager must plan his cultural development as thoughtfully as he plans his work schedule and his profit goals.

I think it's a healthful experience, too, for the executive to ask himself from time to time, honestly and searchingly, "Is the manager functioning at the expense of the man?"

The erosion of the man can be sinister and deadly. I have seen it happen. I can call one man in particular to mind, ambitious, talented, imaginative. He worked long hard hours. He took course after course, steeping himself in systems lore and little else. He never paused long enough to consider how narrow and limited his focus was. And his superior was not sufficiently perceptive, or lacked the proper interest, to point this out to him. In time his talent faded. His imagination dried up. All that remained was the ambition. But it was too late. He had boxed himself into the super-specialist's airtight container. He wound up frustrated and disenchanted, but none the wiser.

Do you have adequate time for random soul searching, mental excursions of self-renewal not directly related to the job?

The head of a large chemical company told me recently, "I regard it as a danger signal if a manager is too busy to think beyond his everyday problems."

A manager I know prides himself on being always in the mainstream of activity. And I mean *always*. He triggers projects. He gets in on the detailed planning stages. He watches personally over each phase like an old mother hen. This executive is project oriented to the point that he is becoming mentally muscle bound. He finds it difficult adjusting his sights to unrelated activities. In truth, he is insecure. He's fearful of getting out of the mainstream and not being missed.

The effects of his outlook are corrosive. It narrows his perspective, undermines his faith in subordinates. It creates an underlying suspiciousness of nature that is difficult to pinpoint but impossible not to sense.

On the other hand, I have been told, a manager has to be realistic. And this is true. The sad fact is that in some organizations you had best stay rooted to the scene of major activity if you do not wish to be squeezed out. Here the disease is not individual but corporate, and it is the fault of the man at the top.

I know of one organization that is a hotbed of political upheaval. The manager too long away from the shop drops down notches on the structural power jack. One executive in this company is a personal friend of mine. He came back recently from a three-month assignment in Europe.

"I left as a key executive and returned feeling like a fifth wheel," he told me. "My place in the political hierarchy had neatly and mysteriously shifted. I had found the European experience broadening and educational. But I decided to take the fruits of my knowledge elsewhere. I found another job."

Smart manager. I think this is another question every executive might well pose to himself from time to time: "Is the climate in my company conducive to cultural enrichment, self-renewal, the broadening of the man as well as the manager?"

It is up to the president to generate and sustain such an atmosphere. If he is lax in fulfilling this responsibility, the alternatives bargained for may be empire building and political patronage.

YOU CAN'T MANUFACTURE THE WILL TO LEARN

It is my suspicion that a situation I can call to mind is not uncommon in U. S. business. The company in question is a medium-size manufacturer of industrial products. For years—until about two years ago—it had a costly and involved system in operation that was loosely referred to as the "management development program."

Actually, the term was a misnomer. The system was fraught with an unbelievable hodgepodge of motivational gimmickry. A prodigious variety of techniques had been structured, most of them designed to impel in managers and supervisors the will to learn, to grow, to advance.

The goal was praiseworthy. But the system had cost a fortune to establish and even more to administer. In my view, it was a vast and colossal waste for the simple reason that true motivation cannot stem from without. It must originate inside the man.

In this case, for each motivational gimmick there was a failure alibi to match. The alibis were concocted, I suspect, more to justify the program than to explain the individual shortcomings inherent in it.

In any event, extensive and complex analyses were made—with the help of attitudinal consultants—in an effort to determine, for example, what caused Smith to walk when he was expected to run. ("His motivational drive is not money, but the desire for increased status." Ergo more experiments.) Or why Johnson was reluctant to respond to the opportunity of a proposed transfer to New York. (It never occurred to the experts that he was comfortably ensconced in a home-grown groove and perfectly content with the status quo.) Or explain Wilson's refusal to take the training required to advance him from research chemist to an administrative post in the lab. (Perhaps he was just a scientist at heart and had no further ambitions.)

Another favorite explanation for "motivational resistance" was age. ("Benson's too old a dog to learn new tricks, and he knows it.")

This, I contend, is the sheerest of nonsense. As Louis Cassels writes in *Nation's Business*: "Modern research has exploded the notion that learning capacity dwindles rapidly as a person ages. It shows that adults can learn effectively at all ages. But it also shows that adults learn in their own way—and this way differs significantly from the way in which children learn."

Some companies attempt to apply children's techniques of motivation to an adult audience, and I don't think it can be done successfully. In any case, this company's program eventually died of its own ineptitude. What much of the motivational gimmickry boils down to, I am convinced, is little more than a series of fads devised by self-styled experts. And I do not mean to imply by this that there is not much good work being done by some of the nation's employee development professionals and attitudinal consultants. My only point is a simple one. The manager who refuses to motivate himself cannot be motivated by others.

A good manager who cares about his people can help to awaken or stimulate the desire to learn. But he cannot *create* it. You cannot force knowledge down people's throats. You can require men to sit through sessions designed to improve their decision-making technique, or help them understand better how to cope with problems, or how to tackle tricky human relations situations. But the only one who will truly benefit from the instruction is the man who would have volunteered for the course, and probably taken it on his own time and at his own expense.

This does not mean to say that industry should not underwrite education. I am all for this, and to the maximum degree possible. But I believe the manager's responsibility is to make the knowledge available to his subordinates, to sharpen awareness, to inspire if he can and, from that point, expect the prospect to take the initiative on his own. For that is the way that people learn.

COMBAT EASY LIVING HABITS

The early American writer Charles Simmons once said, "Good intentions are very mortal and perishable things; like very mellow and choice fruit, they are difficult to keep."

If intentions were the sole criteria for advancement, our nation's corporations would be top heavy with high level officers. In truth, only rarely do the lofty resolutions of men develop into profitable action. As a manager, however, you can make it easier for good intentions to prevail and the "mañana" attitude to fade. Indeed, it is your responsibility to do for the moderately self-motivated subordinate what the super-motivated employee would do on his own. Here are some development techniques that have worked well at North American Rockwell. Hopefully, they will be useful to you as well.

● Identify know-how gaps

Experience has convinced me that even the best of your people can do better if you can spot their know-how weaknesses and help to shore them up. Most people are content to leave well enough alone. But they would be far more content if, instead of leaving well enough alone, they worked hard to make it a little bit better. You can fulfill this objective through a continuing program of testing and evaluation. The idea is to ask the right questions at the right time. Find out what your people don't know that they should know. If nothing else, your questioning approach will create an awareness on their part that what they know is under scrutiny. For the prideful and self-respecting manager, this is usually enough to stir him to corrective action where the need is indicated.

● **Follow up your ideas and suggestions**

An executive I know is highly creative and imaginative. Ideas come to him continuously any time of the day or night. But too often, when he gets an idea, he'll present it to a subordinate with the comment, "Look into this, John," or, "See if you can work it out, Bill." And unless John or Bill comes back to him with his findings, it is likely to slip his mind that he ever brought the subject up. The trouble with this is that his people have come to know his habits. If John or Bill is disinclined to expend the required time and energy on the suggestion, he will relegate it to the pending file. There it will pend and pend and pend. I recently suggested to this executive that he keep a notebook with him, jot down the gist of his ideas and the employees assigned to following them through. After a reasonable time he would then come back to check on the action taken. This would serve two worthwhile purposes: it will break the lassitude of his people; it will keep a wealth of good ideas from going down the drain.

● **Don't settle for easy standards**

Is it fair to expect one employee to produce more than another? "It is grossly unfair," says a prominent industrial psychologist, "to expect otherwise. Human and managerial capabilities vary. Needless to say, expecting any manager to perform beyond his capacities is foolhardy and unrealistic. But encouraging a man to put out less than he can do—because this happens to be the accustomed level of performance—is a disservice to both the individual and the organization."

● **Serve as a disquieting influence**

The self-starter is a precious breed and hard to come by. Chances are, unless your subordinate is highly self-motivated, that he will need an occasional prod from you to keep his performance near peak. In my experience and depending on the nature of the individual, the prod can vary from the very subtle to the near-mandate. Usually your casually voiced suggestion will cause your man to take the hint. Suppose you feel about a subordinate, for example, that his knowledge is insubstantial in a given area of expertise. "Jack," you might say, "do you think linear programming is the answer to our warehouse problem?" Then quickly get him off the hook. Give him a chance to bone up on the subject. Tell him you don't have time to discuss it now, but "Give it some thought. I'd like to go over it with you in the next week or two." If Jack is any manager at all, he'll start cracking books in a hurry.

● **Analyze performance variations**

Knowing that Jones performs job X better than Smith is not enough. Why does he do better? Under what circumstances? Has he always performed better? Has the performance gap remained consistent? Is Smith aware of Jones's superiority? Probing questions of this sort will give you valuable new insights into the strengths and weaknesses of your people. It will help you to determine corrective training measures to take. Where Jones's superiority is due to higher natural intelligence, you may have to live with the situation. But if Smith's performance is lower only on project types A, C, and E, and equal on types B, D, and F, perhaps the nature of his assignments should be altered.

● **Don't settle for satisfactory performance**

A good executive must be a boat rocker from time to time. The chief executive officer of a major airline told me recently, "The manager who is satisfied—or by virtue of his inaction convinces his people he is satisfied—with just passable performance, inspires mediocrity." I have found this to be true. It takes a challenging attitude about approaches, goals, methods, and procedures to keep subordinates on their toes. Those with sufficient ambition and drive will quickly emulate the boss in his dissatisfaction with the status quo. Others, properly prodded, will search for that "better way to do things" out of sheer necessity to keep up with the pack.

● **Strive to emulate and surpass the winners**

Mark Twain once said, "I can live two months on a good compliment."

A manager I know exceeded Twain's performance by a considerable amount. He was, to accord him full credit, a potentially capable executive. But his superior, with every good intention, extolled his virtues to the sky. His motive was to build confidence, but he built it to a point of complacency. The manager became convinced he could do no wrong, that everything he touched turned to gold. As so often happens, the complacency was accompanied by its sidekick, laziness. The manager slid into a serious rut. He failed to explore and examine new techniques. He permitted systems and procedures to outlive their usefulness.

It is true that I can think of few things more important to the management team than the development of confidence among its people. But even this can be overdone. Along with confidence building must go a constant striving to surpass past achievements, to upgrade systems and make them more efficient, to pinpoint successful actions and cash in on them to the maximum.

Experience teaches us that one good way to accomplish this goal is by means of analysis and emulation of what has been done right in one's department, one's company, and one's industry. The trick is to spotlight individual examples of successful profit performance and expand the techniques to as many aspects of the operation as possible.

Case in Point: In Company A, maintenance of non-critical instruments was substantially reduced via a well-planned program of inspection and calibration. The net result was an annual cost saving of $125,000. In Company B, Company A's publicized results and methodology were carefully studied and emulated, with a similar profit gain achieved.

Case in Point: In Company X, executives in one department experimented with recording and taping certain management reports instead of typing them as was formerly done. The experiment met with outstanding success, and was quickly adapted by other departments in the company.

Case in Point: A division of Company M set up a "salesman's idea exchange" to disseminate information about new techniques and sales opportunities. The program was highly successful, and was credited with a substantial increase of business. Other divisions of the company emulated the system with the same degree of success.

Properly analyzed and adapted, there is no reason a winning technique cannot continue to win over and over again. The byproduct benefits of winner-watching are numerous. For one thing, it will accustom your people to the process of continuing change and the need to keep abreast of new developments. It will discourage complacency and keep your organization dynamic. At the same time it will tie in with your confidence-building objectives. From what I have seen, nothing can make a manager feel taller and more important than playing a key role in launching a significant innovation, and receiving the recognition and reward that follows on the heels of such an effort.

In my experience, one good way to watch for winners is by means of the trade press. Thumbing through magazines with profit opportunities in mind can help stir the imagination and produce a wealth of results. I frequently clip items, ads, and whole articles from trade journals and business magazines. I then route the clippings along to the key individual in whom I feel the most constructive action will be triggered. Usually, a short note is attached to the item: "Please evaluate." "Discuss with me." "What do you think?" The little notes, I find, act as excellent thought stimulators. Many new profitable ideas have been generated as a result.

For example, one item I can recall related to the marketing of textile machinery. I passed it along to an executive of the Draper Corporation, a North American Rockwell subsidiary in the textile machinery business. The manager saw no direct application for his own operation. But he shot back a valuable suggestion that was applied with great success in the axle-manufacturing arm of the business. The conclusion is obvious. There is no telling what may result when an imaginative manager's thought wheels start turning.

I find, too, that if the boss makes these little note prods more than a sometime thing, his people will quickly follow suit. In this way, as has been my personal experience, idea mileage can be multiplied throughout the company. What's more, the stimuli will be provided for your subordinates to prod their subordinates as well.

THROW THE TRAINING STRESS ON PROFITS

Oliver Wendell Holmes once said, "Knowledge and timber should not be much used until they are seasoned."

That is true. But like timber, people tend to develop mildew when prematurely exposed to too much weather—mildew of the spirit.

More and more companies are learning that you can train a man to death, particularly a new employee. For years a manufacturer of marine equipment had had an 18-month training program in force. During this period, the trainee followed his veteran salesman mentor about from call to call. The program was designed to teach young engineering graduates the rudiments of salesmanship in this technical field.

The program worked well a decade or two ago. But in recent years the company was finding it increasingly difficult to find qualified trainees, and even more difficult to keep them moored to their apprenticeship role over the long 18-month span. Morale was low, turnover high.

In desperation the company experimented with a one-year training program. This worked better, but not well enough. Further experimentation reduced the program, first to nine months, then to four. Results improved after each experiment. Today, after the four-month period, the trainee's formal apprenticeship is over. He is assigned a limited number of his own accounts, and given full salesman status. Sales objectives at first are relatively simple. The result is that the man is made to feel important. His work becomes more interesting. He is made to sense that he is moving in a forward and positive direction.

Does this mean his education has been curtailed? Not at all. If anything, it expands and intensifies as the boy becomes a man. The training program never stops. He takes courses, attends seminars, participates in problem-solving on the job, observes seasoned veterans as they tackle tough selling challenges and formulate difficult selling decisions. During the initial stages following the four-month apprenticeship period, the new salesman is closely supervised. The counsel and assistance of veteran salesmen and managers are made available to him as his problems increase in complexity. In short, he *learns* while he *does*. As the trainee matures, his responsibilities expand. In time he begins to participate in the training of others.

How well does the revised concept work? Outstandingly well. As a result of this company's revamping of its training tactics and philosophy, turnover among salesmen has been reduced 70 percent. Recruitment has become more successful. It points up, I believe, a developing transition from old-style methods of disseminating knowledge to a more modern and realistic approach.

A nationally known training consultant told me recently: "The trend in many companies is to shed traditional teaching concepts in favor of programs more closely related to stated profit objectives."

Experience tells me that the approach makes sense. Most important, the talented young executive on the rise is apparently all for it.

A young man who, 18 months ago, received his doctorate from Carnegie Tech, today holds down a dynamic managerial post in North American Rockwell's Commercial Products Group. During a recent survey, he remarked:

> You can learn just so much from observing others. The sooner you start doing, the quicker you start building the knowhow and savvy essential for successful management. Profits, I'm rapidly finding out, is the name of the game. When you are given problems to solve and decisions to make that can either boost profits or make them decline, you get a real and practical insight into what business is all about. It's the kind of knowledge that you can't acquire very well on a second-hand basis.

This young man's approach to business augurs well for his future success. In our operation we do our best to tie training objectives into profit objectives, and we find that the effort pays off. I mean practically and realistically, not on a "blue sky" basis. We will evaluate a specific training program, for example, in terms of its ability to cut scrap by six percent, or absence by fifteen percent, or selling expenses by twelve percent, or the incidence of errors by thirty percent. Or by its ability to increase the flow of suggestions by twenty-five percent.

At various phases during and after the program, we assess actual results against the estimated results. If the program lives up to specifically stated expectations, or shows promise of living up to them in the future, we will perpetuate it. Otherwise, down the drain it goes, and new approaches will be tried.

TUNE IN TO THE TIMES

A surprising number of companies like the marine equipment manufacturer, are using the same methods to train their people today as they did five, seven, and ten years ago. How closely are your company's training methods in tune with the times? Educational breakthroughs during the past decade or so have been impressive. Some have produced dramatically successful results in situations where the innovation and the training requirement were properly matched. Sometimes the gain is in the form of reduced training costs; other times in the form of faster learning, better comprehension, longer retention. And as often as not the gain consists of a combination of both lower costs and better learning results.

Has your company cashed in on modern training techniques introduced during the past ten to fifteen years? Hopefully, the following questionnaire will help you to evaluate your current program. The more "Yes" answers you can provide to the questions that follow, the greater the likelihood that your company is indeed in tune with the times, at least so far as its educational tactics are concerned.

1. Have your training methods and concepts changed significantly within the past five years? _____

2. Have you expanded your educational program beyond technical and product requirements to include such skills as management decision-making, problem-solving and handling of human relations situations? _____

3. Have you reappraised within the past three years the value of programmed teaching concepts in response to your company's training needs? _____

4. Has investigation convinced you that formal classroom instruction is a relatively uneconomical and inefficient way to solve many training requirements? _____

5. Does your company employ a variety of teaching methods— often in combination within the same program—to impart new skills to your people? _____

6. Does the concept of learning by doing play a vital role in your training program and philosophy? _____

7. Does your company work with the university to initiate new subjects, structure new courses, and make them more compatible with the requirements of your company and industry? _____

8. Does your company, within financial and time limitations, provide financial and moral

support for the university?

_____

9. Do you stimulate your peoples' desire to learn by tying career advancement to the advancement of knowledge?

_____

10. Do you set a proper example for your people by wearing proudly and prominently your own "Hat of the Student?"   _____

11. Do you make it easy and attractive for your people to perpetuate their business education by means of a generous tuition refund program, in-plant training sessions, information dissemination through company communications channels, availability to trade publications and library materials, etc.?

_____

12. Have you cut down on the travel and hotel bills relating to your training program by investigating methods which bring the program to the student—programmed instruction, video tape, etc.—instead of transporting the student to the program?   _____

13. Have you fully explored the use of video tape in its various combinations—tape and slide presentations, tape/telephone conference techniques, etc.—in response to your company's training requirements?   _____

14. Do you continually appraise and reappraise the effectiveness of your training program by measuring expected student performance against actual results achieved?

_____

SCHEDULE THE TRAINING TO COINCIDE WITH THE APPLICATIONS OF KNOWLEDGE

A medium-size wholesaler of liquors and wines planned a new data processing installation to start operating in January after the closeout of the year. The company took advantage of its summer lull to send six of its people to school to learn how to operate the machines, handle the cards, and wire the plugboards. As the company learned to its dismay, the plan was ill timed and extremely costly.

As often happens, the installation setup operations fell behind schedule. The starting date was advanced from January 3rd to March 1st. By this time two of the six employees trained had left the company. The other four recalled little of what they had been taught, although three of the four had received higher than average grades.

Almost from the start of the operation, it was in trouble. Only the supervisor was experienced. The four trained employees tried their hardest, worked long extra hours, and expended their full energies to make the system work. But their ineptitude could not be surmounted. Error upon error caused chaos and confusion. In the end, two experienced men had to be hired and a consultant called in to help unravel the mess and restructure the operation.

The lesson is clear. Adults learn most effectively by putting the knowledge to work as soon as possible after it has been acquired. The more often and quickly the application is repeated, the better the rate of retention will be. Within one year the trainee forgets 50 percent of what he has learned if the knowledge has not been put to use, according to *Nation's Business*. After two years the loss of retention is 80 percent. In this case, it was estimated the four employees forgot about 60 percent of what they had been taught within an eight-month period. This might indicate that the more technical the instruction, the lower the retention rate if not applied.

The swift application of all kinds of knowledge is crucial, especially in the case of management development.

Says the training director of a major oil company:

> Better retention isn't the only reason knowledge should be used soon after it is imparted. The learner has more respect for instruction when he can see its practical application looming up before him. Training that is not directly related to operations is often taken casually and regarded as irrelevant. To the intelligent manager, training implies a promise to broader opportunity and responsibility, and the eventual reward that goes with it.

TRAIN FOR TOMORROW

A chief executive with his sights set on growth educates himself and his people with one eye on today, the other on the future.

Carnegie Tech Professor Harold J. Leavitt predicts that by 1980, highly creative people will take over the top management of American companies. They will hold master's or doctorate degrees in business, in science, in the arts.

But education in college, I have found, is only a beginning. The technical knowledge acquired there may be a man's chief asset during his first five years out of school. But the curve tends to flatten as technology changes and as demands are made on the manager for skills in human relations, in problem solving, and in decision-making as well as technical areas.

Obviously, the engineer who graduated ten years ago would be in an impossible situation today if he had only his ten-year-old knowledge. By the same token, today's graduate would be in an impossible situation if he attempted to make do with today's knowledge ten years from now.

Today's manager and scientist cannot afford to stop the process of education. Should he do so, he would soon find himself working with obsolete ideas and out-of-date information, struggling to master equipment whose language is unfamiliar to him and whose function he does not understand.

This is particularly true in areas of technology. "Scientific knowledge is constantly changing," said the American author and critic James T. Adams. "A discovery of one year receives confirmation the next or is thrown aside."

These words were written about 30 years ago. Consider by what factor the impact of the statement might be multiplied by today. The mere prospect of new technological developments in the next ten or so years is enough to stun the imagination.

We may guess, but we can't be sure, what these developments may be. Likely to be included are startling innovations in various phases of automation and cybernation. They may involve the use of laser beams in communications. Or transmission of electricity without wires. Or the enlargement of voiced communications between computer and man. Or the use of holograms to produce truly three-dimensional movies, television, and radar pictures— pictures where you will be able to move your head to one side, change your perspective, and see the side of the object or other objects behind the first that were hidden in the straight-on view.

A manager must live and work with the sure knowledge that many of our latest and most advanced machines are now in their Model T stage, compared to what they will be in the not-too-distant future.

In their remarkable book, *The Year 2000—A Framework For Speculation* (Macmillan, 1967), authors Herman Kahn and Anthony Wiener estimate that over the past 15 years, the basic criterion of computer performance has increased by a factor of ten every two or three years. They point out that we are beginning to reach limits set by basic physical constraints, such as the speed of light; and so we may not be able to duplicate this performance in the future. Yet one company is using radically new circuitry and storage concepts to develop a remarkable new computer system. This is expected to provide speeds several hundred times that of existing speeds, and more than a hundred times faster than any other computer known to be in development. The point is that the class of 1975 or 1980 will be familiar with hardware of this kind. The working manager or scientist must be equally familiar with it if he is to compete successfully with his peers and with the new crop of managers being produced by the nation's colleges.

This is not without good reason that a corporation's educational program rates high on the list of "fringe benefits" for the thoughtful and well-informed graduate who wishes to make business his career.

CHAPTER EIGHT

The Hat of the Reporter

Corporate life these days is life in a fishbowl. The news media are alert and extremely knowledgeable. When activities of significance take place in a company of some size, they want to know about them. And they have ways of finding out whether you want to tell them or not. Your best bet, therefore, is to tell them.

This doesn't imply, of course, that you should blurt out intimate business details indiscriminately to anyone who asks. Obviously, certain research and technological information, or marketing plans and the like, that would be of strategic value to competitors must remain closely guarded corporate secrets. That's not the type of intelligence I have in mind. What I'm referring to is the information that is meaningful and important to people with a personal stake in the progress of your company. In short, all of your various "publics."

Until fairly recently many companies were rather closemouthed about their plans and goals as a matter of corporate policy. Twenty-five, fifteen, even ten years ago, it was not uncommon to hear a chief executive say, "We've got the right to conduct our business as we wish, and the way we do business is nobody else's business."

Times have changed. Today the president who sits high up in

his ivory tower and disdainfully considers his organization immune to public opinion is living in the past. He jeopardizes his company and casts doubts on its reputation. Today, in many circles and on many issues, silence is regarded as evidence of guilt.

Today, if you run a publicly-owned corporation, the way you conduct your business is almost literally everybody's business. And I can tell you from personal experience that the Hat of the Reporter—a truthful, accurate, conscientious reporter—is one of the most important items in the presidential wardrobe.

DEFINE YOUR PUBLICS

A company president I know told me recently:

> I've been reviewing our history, Al, and we've come through a real metamorphosis. Ten years ago if a newspaperman called on me, wanting to know about some proposed new plant, or our acquisition policy, or something else in the works, chances are he would have received precious little information he could use. Seven years ago he would have found me much less reluctant to talk. Four years ago he wouldn't have had to come to us; we would have gotten to him first. Today? Well, our information dissemination process is refined to the point where we disperse news, not only willingly, but on a highly specialized basis. And instead of suffering from our frankness as I once feared, I find it's helping us to get cooperation and support which I wouldn't have believed possible ten years ago.

What this executive is saying is that his company's policy is now one of free and frank disclosure, and that its various publics have been defined in a way that makes such disclosure easier and more effective. I couldn't agree more that there is no other way for a major corporation to operate today.

I can remember back several years in my own organization, Rockwell-Standard Corporation, long before the merger with North American Aviation, when we too thought in terms of only one generalized public. Even today, some presidents continue to think this way. Sooner or later, I'm sure, they'll discover what a grave mistake this is. Today's growing corporation must reach a variety of audiences. Each requires—and is entitled to—individualized treatment and specific types of information. For example:

- **Employees**

Vital changes—acquisitions, expansion, plant closings, automation, etc.—are of prime concern to employees on all levels. As one
consultant says, "It's bad business when employees hear important news via the grapevine or press instead of from their own
management." I've found this to be true. If you level with your
people, they will come to know in time that your word is to be
trusted. If they get their information secondhand, at worst it will
be distorted or totally untrue, and at best they will misinterpret
the data. Personally, I consider it a prime presidential responsibility to see to it that employees are given the facts squarely,
honestly, and in time.

- **Shareholders**

No law states that you can't take the hardnosed approach to
business and be truthful at the same time. The simple reality is
that the growth of your stock will in large measure determine
your ability to raise capital to advance your profit goals. And the
attitudes and opinions of your shareholders will greatly influence
the price of your stock. Thus it follows that if you keep your
shareholders properly and truthfully informed about the key
issues that concern them, you will sustain their confidence and
good will. That's why I am a great believer in interim statements:
flash reports and the like. I think it's important that your shareholders receive significant news about your business before it
appears in the press, and in some cases before it appears in your
quarterly report.

- **Financial community**

Keeping the financial community currently abreast of major
corporate aims and developments is effective in a variety of ways.
For one thing, bankers, brokers, and investment specialists are
prime movers of stock. For another, these are the men who hold
the purse strings. I'll cite an example. Rockwell-Standard, as you
may know, prior to the merger was a leading producer of automotive parts. Yet auto parts sales constituted a minor percentage
of our business and whenever analysts predicted a decline in auto
sales, we went out of our way to get this fact across to the financial community. The communications effort paid off. As one

banker told me, "Much of your stock would have been dumped otherwise." Straightforward liaison with the financial community has its byproduct benefits as well. I recall one instance where a Rockwell-Standard division borrowed money from a New York bank for one-half percent less than was charged a company twice its size. The head of the larger company wanted to know why it didn't qualify for the better rate. The answer he got was simple and blunt. "We know all that we need to know about the Rockwell group. Certain aspects of your operation are a little bit hazy." The point is clear. When you level with people, you go beyond gaining recognition; you build a trust.

● **Local community**

Primarily, as a member of the community, it's your duty to strengthen and protect it. Second, to exist successfully within the community, you will need the confidence and support of its citizens and officials. For one thing, you rely on the community for your labor supply. You deal with its producers of products and services. To some extent you're dependent on its health, sanitation, safety, and protection services. You need its cooperation in matters of traffic and construction. When any action that could affect the economy and well-being of local residents is anticipated, it is good business, as well as moral sense, to provide full and honest disclosure. Thus you can optimize opportunities and minimize the adverse effect of unfavorable news such as cutbacks or plant closings.

● **Customers**

To customers, direct or indirect, you owe your existence. It thus becomes a key presidential obligation to see to it that no customer is ever left in an untenable position as a result of a policy decision. One of our earliest moves at North American Rockwell, when a major decision is made, is to ask: "How will this affect our customers?" And, "How will they react to the decision?" Sometimes you may know that the proposed action will not adversely affect the customer in any way. Still it is important for you to consider how *he* will interpret the move. I recall one instance where a warehouse was closed by a company because it had found a faster and more economical way to distribute its products. This knowledge was not shared by some customers, however, who assumed that the discontinued warehouse would mean a lowering of service standards. As a result, complaints poured in and business dropped off. It all could have been avoided with a good, simple, and inexpensive communications program.

● **Suppliers**

Suppliers depend on your operation as much as you depend on theirs. The same philosophy that applies to customers applies to suppliers: "How will they be affected? How will they respond?" Some years ago a company I know purchased a smaller company that made evaporators, heat exchangers, filters, and other products. The company intended to retain and expand the evaporator and heat exchanger business, and sell off other operations. But a prime supplier who had long furnished the company with filters was unaware of its intention. They naturally assumed that this customer would soon start producing its own special-purpose filters and that the account would eventually dry up. As a result, service dropped off. Salesmen stopped calling. Delivery performance declined. Five months and about a hundred complaints later, the truth came out, and the good relationship was reinstated. But again, the simple expedient of communicating intentions effectively would have staved off a good deal of aggravation, loss, and waste.

DIG FOR TRUTH

Thomas Jefferson once said, "It is rare that the public sentiment decides immorally or unwisely, and the individual (or company) who differs from it ought to distrust and examine well his own opinion."

What he neglected to mention, of course, is that first you must read public sentiment accurately. From what I have observed, digging for the truth is no simple task. It takes time, wisdom, and patience.

Steer clear of quick assumptions

As often as not, the story a company wants to convey to its public is triggered by a particular problem or need that develops. The big danger, I have found, is to base your message on what you *assume* your public thinks and feels rather than what you *know with reasonable certainty* your public thinks and feels.

One company had decided to make certain drastic changes in its service organization and methods of distribution. It wisely preceded the innovation with a program designed to sell customers on the idea. The campaign was efficiently organized and smoothly executed. Top professional writers were retained to prepare a series of newsletters and brochures explaining the new system. The effort shaped up well and those involved beamed and congratulated each other. Response from the field, however, was anything but enthusiastic. As a result (after the fact), an outside organization was called in to sample customer sentiment.

The answers fed back had a sobering effect on management. No one was critical of the professional quality of the campaign. This, in fact, was a major problem. Customers were apprehensive. The proposed changes had a major bearing on their business, and they weren't convinced. The campaign was *too* professional, many customers felt, although they didn't express it in so many words. It was too slick, too glib, too impersonal. As a result, credibility was missing. One customer said, "They're trying to ram a bill of goods down my throat. Frankly, I don't know how some of these changes will work out for me."

All that was really needed here was some human personal contact. The written materials were fine—but not without a follow-through by salesmen calling on the accounts, explaining the system, answering questions, assuaging doubts.

The conclusion is clear. A desire to transmit your story and shape public opinion based on its merits is not enough. You must first find out, "What shape?" This is particularly true when the winds of adverse opinion appear to be blowing your way. Unless your anemometer is precisely set, you may wind up beating the breeze with a feather. How can you accurately test the wind? Professional public relations people are familiar with the various techniques which range from questionnaire surveys and depth interviews to freeform discussions conducted on an informal basis.

Put salesmen on your research team

But hold on before you shell out a large sum on an attitudinal study, particularly if customers are involved. This may be another job for your salesman-intelligence force. I've seen instances where a well-aimed salesmen's probe accomplished more in the way of uncovering the root cause behind anticompany sentiment than an external effort taking twice as long and costing three times as much could have done.

In one medium-sized company a sudden drop in business created management concern. The problem was studied and the conclusion reached that the slide was a result of recent labor difficulties, now settled. In short order, it was expected, sales would pick up again. But they didn't pick up. They grew worse. Management apprehension grew. The president was advised to call in a consulting firm, reshape the sales organization, change the product line, and whatnot. He took none of this advice. Instead he selected 50 accounts where business had dropped off noticeably, and instructed salesmen to talk with these customers and find out why.

What they learned was that a rumor stemming from an unidentified source had been circulated in the field: "We've heard you're getting ready to sell out to a big eastern outfit." It was nonsense, of course. Salesmen who previously had heard the rumor, had checked back at the office, were assured it was without foundation, and promptly dismissed it from their minds. But customers were not so easily convinced.

They were deeply troubled because the company ran a franchised operation with selected and controlled distribution. The new company, rumor had it, would go hogwild on distribution, shooting for a mass market and discontinuing franchise arrangements. As a result, many customers formerly loyal started shifting allegiance and switching to competitive lines.

When the true reason for the decline was disclosed, all it took was an intensive communications campaign—targeted at the bull's eye, not the barn—to set the picture straight.

I've seen the same pattern repeated time and again. The place to measure public opinion accurately is right on the scene—in the market-place, among your employees, in conversation with businessmen and leading officials—depending on which of your publics is involved. In short, I've learned one thing. You cannot effectively gauge the attitudes of people comfortably ensconced in your swivel chair with a speculative look in your eye.

PREPARE FOR THE WORST

Theodore Roosevelt once said, "You never have trouble if you are prepared for it." This could be stretching a point, but in general I have found it to be true.

If catastrophe were to hit your company tomorrow, would you be ready for it? Unpleasant prospect, to be sure. But it could happen. Fire could break out, an explosion erupt. You read about such tragedies every day. Industrial accident can cause people to be injured, burned, drowned, poisoned, asphyxiated. As any newspaper editor will tell you, these things happen. You exercise every conceivable precaution to keep them from happening. But still, you can never be sure.

It's a thought for a president to ponder. If sudden tragedy were to strike, what would you do? Would you know what to tell the press, the community, the relatives of victims? Would you be qualified to act with the reasonable assurance, coolheadedness, and control expected of a chief executive? Or would you hit the panic button and respond in a way you might regret for years?

What I am saying may seem a bit harsh, even macabre. And I'm not suggesting that you concoct a public relations kit to deal with catastrophe. On the other hand, I have heard more than one president mutter remorsefully after an harrowing experience, "Why weren't we prepared for this?"

That's why I think it would serve your company and yourself well to have in readiness—if and when you need it—a carefully thoughtout procedure for dealing with disaster, and also with such occurrences as strikes, plant shutdowns, and defalcations as well. What you draw up need not be very specific; its main aim is to pre-set your communications machinery so that it can be put into effective motion as quickly after the event as possible.

Why prepare for the worst? For a variety of reasons. For one thing, it is when crisis occurs that the press and other media turn swiftly to the chief executive for information and explanations. People want to know what happened and why. They want to know what will happen as a result, and what are the next moves you expect to make. And they want to know it *now*—in time for the next broadcast, or the next edition.

Why is preparation essential? Because it is a time when seven

editors will be trying simultaneously to reach you. It is a time
when subordinates are looking to you for guidance and direction. It is a time when all eyes are focused in your direction. It
is a time when it becomes especially vital that your story be
told honestly and in the most favorable light possible. It is a
time when you are eager to squash rumors and cool panic, when
you cannot afford to make a mistake. And most of all, it's a time
when you simply do not have the hours for everything that needs
to be done.

If such a pre-planned communications program accomplishes
nothing else, it will help to buy you time. It will also rout confusion. You'll be working from a carefully worked-out procedure,
not playing it by ear. This can save you money as well as time.
In one company where no such program had been set up, an
explosion took two lives and destroyed a half-million dollars
worth of facilities. The president appeared at a hastily called
press conference. Pressed for information, he emotionally cast
aspersions on a contracting firm, honestly believing at the time
that this organization was to blame for the tragedy. A subse-
quent libel suit cost the company $350,000. It is a hard way to
learn that impulse action at time of disaster does not pay off.
Preparation would help to prevent such an occurrence.

What should your preparation include? It might specify which
of your lieutenants could speak for you in your absence. It would
spell out in general what statements would have to be made, and
to whom. It would outline a procedure for investigating an accident, and another for conducting officials and representatives of
the press to any disaster area. It would provide for the careful
wording of initial statements with legal considerations in mind.
It might even designate specific individuals for such tasks as
writing and speaking, so that at the actual time of emergency,
delegation would be swift and effective.

Needless to say, specific actions and statements must be tai-
lored to the situation at hand. But having procedures to work
from is a good deal easier than attempting to organize a program during a period that is hectic and trying for all involved.

Case in point

What about such events as strikes and plant shutdowns? However you try to avoid them, they happen in the best of com-

panies. Here, of course, you can become more specific in your planning. What, for example, should a communications program consist of if a plant closing is on the horizon? The question was posed to North American Rockwell by *Business Management* magazine. Here in brief is the procedure we follow:

1. Establish a network of effective in-plant management communications. It's important that plant management, labor relations, public relations people, and others concerned work together to scotch false rumors and prevent anything but the facts from emerging.
2. Prepare statements that are geared to answer press inquiries—particularly inquiries stemming from leaks before official announcements are made.
3. Prepare official statements for employees, the union, and the press well in advance of their actual release. Doing this on a crash basis can be risky, in terms of omitted thoughts and imprecise wording.
4. Prepare statements that are geared to answer inquiries from community officials and businessmen, whether premature or not.
5. Set up a program to keep customers informed and to avoid any possible interruption of customer operation.
6. Prepare letters to government leaders. The size and importance of the plant is a major factor here. It is particularly critical in a small town where economic dependency on the plant is a key issue. ,
7. Prepare letters for suppliers, customers, employees, and executives at other locations.

Please note that in such preparation, not one but all of the company's publics are taken into careful consideration.

CASH IN ON PERSONAL APPEAL

It has been my experience that many communications programs fail for the same reason many sales programs fail. They're too pat, too obviously "packaged," too patently impersonal.

Aristotle once offered sound advice to all men who wish to get their message across: "Think like a wise man, but communicate in the language of the people." The most effective "language of the people," I'm convinced, is the kind you transmit flexibly and informally on a face-to-face basis. Busy as I am, I consider it of the utmost importance to meet personally with as many of my people as I can any time a major corporate change is in the offing. If a new company is acquired, for example, or an important new product developed, I make it a point to stroll from department to department at corporate headquarters at least, and discuss the subject in an informal edge-of-the-desk way.

I cannot over-emphasize the value I personally derive from such exchanges. For one thing, it keeps me in close touch with employees at all levels. It gives them the opportunity to fire questions, offer suggestions, and air any apprehensions that might exist. And it gives me a personal charge as well. Because when you're perched on that desk and leveling with the people who work for you and with you, you can tell instinctively from the reception you get whether they are with you or not. It also helps to avoid a pitfall I find all too common in most companies today. A president can become so mired by the facts and figures ground out by computers that he forgets the main commodity with which his company deals is not widgets, but human beings.

MAKE EVERYBODY A PUBLIC RELATIONS MAN

The editor of a nationally known management magazine recently jokingly described North American Rockwell as "the company with the PR staff of thousands." Tongue in cheek, or not, I was flattered by the remark. What he alluded to was a practice we encourage at every opportunity. That's the strategy of getting as many of your key people as possible to disseminate the corporate message in the community and over their particular areas of contact. The concept is simple. If you can successfully enlist the support and enthusiasm of your subordinates for your programs and objectives, you are a short step away from spreading the word.

The next move is to encourage your top aides and middle managers to go out into the community with your company's story on a face-to-face basis. The fact is that most people today —the so-called influentials especially—are so inundated with information from a myriad of sources, it is often difficult to get your message heard through all the competing "noise." It helps

immeasurably, I have found, if you can tell your story in a re-
freshingly personal way that gives the audience a chance to ask
questions and exchange ideas. In short, what applies for the
president, applies for his key people as well.

One good way of getting into the community with your story
is to set up a speakers bureau. The idea is not a new one. As
Business Management explains: "In speaking publicly, your middle managers will not only render a service to your community,
but also build good will for your company. What's more, they'll
help ready themselves for top executive posts."

One caution, however: I cannot stress too strongly the importance of making sure your own people are *sold* on your message before attempting to carry it outside. As *Nation's Business*
points out: "The power of person-to-person communication rests
in the personal conviction of the person speaking. Unfortunately,
the way employees feel about a company often falls short of
management's expectations." Sometimes, of course, this is as
much the fault of the company as of the disenchanted manager.
And though an expanded PR force can serve well to strengthen
your communications program, it makes good sense, before sending a "good will ambassador" into the field, to assess the extent
of his good will.

RIGHT OR WRONG? IT'S THE PRESIDENT'S JOB TO DECIDE

It is the avowed policy of most public-minded companies,
when compelled to shut down an unprofitable plant, to make
every possible effort to help employees find new jobs. No one
would dispute the justice of, or the need for, such a program.
But unhappily, in many companies stated policy and actual practice are miles apart. Where matters of conscience are involved,
it becomes the president's responsibility to spot such disparity
and take steps to remove it.

A close friend who is head of a major corporation recently told
me that, while in the throes preceding a plant shutdown, he was
handed the draft of a news release to approve. It was written
by the public relations department. It was well organized and
professionally written with the apparent purpose of selling the
company's social conscience to the press by outlining its great
concern for the people who would lose their jobs as a result of
the shutdown.

My friend's response was blunt. "The prose is smooth and glib, but I'm not personally convinced that we're doing as much for these people as we claim to be doing." He then demanded a definitive report describing exactly what was being done, what it cost, and what results were expected.

The report confirmed his doubts. "The lip service is there," he told his PR aide, "but I'm not satisfied with the evidence." He thereupon took steps to enlarge and intensify the re-employment program.

The point is clear. Where matters of corporate conscience are involved, it's the president's task to set the pace. It is a responsibility he cannot in good conscience delegate to PR people or anyone else.

A corporation vice president of PR stated the case in *The Public Relations Quarterly*:

> The role of the public relations department as a public conscience is lessening and its role as expert communications technicians is gaining ground. I think this is due to several factors. For one thing, the people who are selected for increased managerial responsibility have been chosen by a process which has included, over the years, appraisals of a man's ability to follow his own conscience. Also, our management people have been not only trained but in part have been selected for their sensitivity in this area of what the public wants and what the public expects from us. My personal experience is that in the line operation, you know pretty well what is expected of you and what the public goals are. We have a carefully nurtured and trained management which I really don't think requires a hired conscience. Nevertheless, I think public relations men perhaps still see themselves, in many cases, as useful corporate consciences.

I think these thoughts are worth pondering by chief executives of companies large and small. The questions to soul-search are, first, "Are you as chief executive personally and aggressively making the key 'Right or wrong?' decisions in your company, and not delegating the task?" And second, "Are your lieutenants properly sensitive to decisions of conscience in their own areas of operation?"

DON'T SUBSTITUTE GIMMICKRY FOR HONESTY

"Tricks aren't worth the trouble," writes the head of a nationally known PR firm in *Business Management* magazine, "and it never pays to substitute words for ideas and honesty."

He tells the story of a financial consultant who was interviewed by a number of important editors. Each time he answered questions with candor, sometimes admitting weaknesses in his own service and his field as a whole. Later one of his associates advised him to be a little less candid, a little more glib with the press.

"If I have to make up facts in order to get my picture in the paper," he replied, "it isn't worth it."

The man's honesty paid off. The editors, appreciating his straight answers, have continued to call him for statements and mention his name over a period of years. Some executives, adds the PR executive, treat press people like dopes or second class citizens. Other executives treat them with too much solicitousness. Either can be self-defeating. The best advice: treat the press like people. That way you just cannot go wrong.

I couldn't agree more with this philosophy of communicating with the public and dealing with the press. I have seen public relations gimmickry backfire again and again. But I cannot recall a single instance where either I or any other top-level officer, ever told the truth on a man-to-man basis and lived to regret it.

DARE TO BE DIFFERENT

Thomas Carlyle once said, "The merit of originality is not novelty; it is sincerity. The believing man is the original man; whatsoever he believes, he believes it for himself, not for another."

If I had my way, I would make this statement into a sign and hang one on the wall of every advertising and PR office in the nation. Daring to be different, in my view, is by far the most effective form of communication.

An enlightened advertising executive told me recently:

> I'm tired of hearing professional ad and PR men spout how important it is that people know the truth about the client's products and services, policies, and objectives. That's right, of course. But they're equally entitled not to be bored to death in the process.

In my opinion, boring the people you are trying to reach effectively makes about as much sense as trying to lure customers with a promise of higher prices. Boredom is a stone's throw from disenchantment.

Increasingly, I believe, the advertising and public relations community is coming to appreciate the importance of genuine and uncontrived originality in its communications. William F. May, chief executive of American Can Company, recently gave an address before the Association of Industrial Advertisers. Among his remarks:

> A retired executive of one of our agencies has put the whole proposition as directly and appropriately as I've ever heard it. He said: "The beginning of greatness is to be different. Conversely, the beginning of mediocrity is to be the same. Similarity flourishes like weeds. But differences must be cultivated like rare and fragile flowers. The successful production of great advertising is a never-ending resistance to similarity; a constant struggle to avoid the usual; a continuous effort to provide new ideas, to illustrate them with freshness, and to express them with originality."

Mr. May went on to point out:

> Considering that more than 2000 advertisements a day will be directed to Americans by 1970, selectivity will be very high. The public might do well to paraphrase Francis Bacon's comment on books to fit the situation: Some advertisements are to be tasted, others to be swallowed, and some few to be chewed and digested.

Mention this to the next advertising executive you meet, and the chances are his response will be an enthusiastic, "Hear, hear!" But from my experience in this area, the president's Reporter's Hat should be worn at a slightly suspicious angle. Philip H. Dougherty puts it this way in the *New York Times*: "Advertisers are all looking for the so-called creative agencies and there are people on their phones constantly looking for an account and saying they are hot and creative." Quoting an unnamed advertiser, he adds, "For every creative agency there are ten fakes doing gimmick ads for the sake of doing them."

Sometimes, from what I have seen, it becomes the task of the chief executive to sift the evidence and differentiate between the phonies in the business and the truly creative producers.

YOUR PRESS PASS

One final note to keep in your hat brim when you're wearing the Hat of the Reporter. Have some worthwhile things besides profits to tell people about. It's your responsibility as chief executive not only to tell your company's story but also to make sure that story is worth telling.

Is your company really doing its share as a corporate citizen? The question calls for some soul-searching.

Another question—perhaps the great one of our times: Are you willing to lose a competitive edge by being the first in your area to add expensive dust collectors or water treatment facilities or noise-suppression devices in your plant? I warn you that there is no easy answer to the question.

Beyond that, have you considered a possible role for your company in active pollution control, for profits? Recently we decided that there could be no better use for some of our patents and experience than in helping to develop anti-pollution technology. So we helped to form a new company called Envirotech Corporation. Our hope and belief is that this company and others like it will not only prove profitable but also will materially contribute toward making our planet habitable for generations to come.

If you, as a president, believe in corporate citizenship, you'll watch what you say to the public. To be specific:

Don't make speeches about cleaning up the environment unless you're really trying to do something about it.

Don't sound off about the quality of life unless you're sure all your plants are healthful, decent, invigorating places in which to work.

Don't talk about the responsibility of business to the community unless you've got some talented people actually at work on problems like transportation and housing.

Don't issue pronouncements on employee self-fulfillment unless that is your active, everyday personnel policy.

And as for you as a private human being, don't make speeches about the duty of businessmen to lead unless you take stands, serve on working committees, patronize and encourage the arts, help to build universities, extend aid to small businessmen. . . . And you can complete your own list.

CHAPTER NINE

The Hat of the Coach of Champions

You can take your choice. The simple little cap at the top of the page might be the one worn by Vince Lombardi all those winning years at Green Bay. Or if you prefer baseball, make it the cap of Casey Stengel or Leo Durocher. In just about any sport, the coach or manager has one of these caps that he wears in games or practice sessions. And in just about any sport, the great preoccupation of the man in charge is to get every man to play the game as well as it is humanly possible for him to play it.

What makes a champion? A very few seem to have been born with it. Most athletes, however, have to learn their trade like anyone else. Then at some point in their careers the magic thing happens and they suddenly can "put it all together." Usually the coaching is responsible. The player is lucky enough to be toiling for a coach who can observe, correct, explain, cajole, threaten, and inspire him to reveal every ounce of skill he possesses.

What I am talking about, of course, is motivation. Earlier, in Chapter 4, I discussed the good basic approach to motivation that a president uses as the Impresario of his company, bringing together men and ideas. Now I'd like to go a step further.

I'd like to put things on a strictly individual basis. How do you "build a fire" under a man—not just any man but one real human being? Because that's what a president must do with the men in his immediate circle and, by implication, with everyone in the company (and a great many people outside it). You've got to light a steady flame in each man that will not be extinguished when the storm clouds roll in, but will burn all the more brightly in a crisis or a moment of inspiration.

And here's where I part company with quite a few outstanding, highly successful executives who believe in a more or less get-tough, hard-line management approach. They attempt to motivate through fear. They are authoritarian and disciplinarian. They harass the troops. And those who have a certain charisma find that this kind of leadership works. I know one corporation president who simply doesn't believe in letting up on the pressure. The other day, when a new distribution center was opened a month ahead of schedule, he growled at his engineers because, he said, with all the good weather and other breaks they'd had, they should have finished the project two months early.

As I said, that kind of thing works for him. But it's not my style. And I don't think it would work for most executives.

Not that I've never chewed out anyone. I have, on occasion, such as when a divisional executive failed to return the required percentage on stockholder equity in his operations, for no good and valid reason. But when at all possible—and that means most of the time—I prefer to do my blaze-kindling a completely different way. For instance:

—I often issue generally worded memos that cause people to scratch their heads and wonder just what in the world I could have meant.

—And I'm occasionally late for appointments because I stopped to chat with perfect strangers.

—And, of course, I fraternize shamelessly with third and fourth level subordinates.

None of these things are done, however, through absent-mindedness or lack of exposure to management principles. They are done intentionally, on a controlled basis, with a clear goal in mind. This is the way I "coach" employees and others, and I think the same methods will work for you.

The fact is that the old order in management is changing, and changing rapidly. Cherished concepts are crumbling. No longer is money the prime motivator for all employees. No longer is a manager promoted mainly because of what he can do in his special field. No longer is the pyramid widely regarded as the best of all possible business structures. Even the importance of decision-making itself has come under scrutiny in the light of new and more democratic business organizations.

"Permissiveness management," some call it. The idea is to get the participation of the group, even in some decisions. Well, these theories are fine, but it seems to me that what they often do is formalize what a good manager does anyway. He stays cool, in my opinion, and leads with neither the carrot nor the stick, but with the mind-prodder—in my case, among other things, the generalized memo.

Does the phrase bother you? Well, let's explain what I mean. Just the other day I grabbed a piece of interoffice memo paper, addressed it by hand, and deliberately wrote: "Suggest staff research on this project may be rather too exhaustive. Moderation in all things." The memo went to one of our vice presidents, and as I later was told, it drove him crazy. He read my little cryptograph, read it over again, then tried reading it backwards. Finally he couldn't stand it any longer so he stopped in at my office and asked me if I'd mind telling him what it was I had in mind.

"Well, what do you think it meant?" I asked gently.

He could see I wasn't going to elaborate further so he went back with at least the general impression that I wanted him to delve deeper into the problem—not my memo, but the business problem it concerned. After a while he got the message—that his project task force had spent too much time marshalling tons of background information and not enough time doing hard creative thinking. The research, in other words, was too exhaustive. What happened then was that the vice president got the message as I knew he would, switched gears, and got the project off the ground.

Why didn't I just tell him what I wanted? What did I gain by this oblique approach? Simple. I made him think for himself. And when he saw things my way, he saw them *his* way, too, with the excitement of personal discovery. "You can't hire a hand," said Temple Burling, a famous labor relations professor of Cornell University, "but must hire the whole man." It applies to a manager as truly as to a workman. It's the whole man you must get on your side, and I've found that indirection is one good way to do it.

Before we go any further, however, let's get down to some cases. Here are some situations of the kind faced by any corporate president who wants to get the best out of his "players." There's no one right or wrong answer. But I do have my own definite ideas about what should be done in each. See if you and I agree.

CASE NUMBER 1: THE RELUCTANT DRAGON

Your research chief, a walking encyclopedia in the technical line, does a consistently good job. But you're not satisfied. In meetings with other executives he doesn't have enough to say. He's holding back. You're not sure whether it's modesty or the fact that he doubts that those other guys would understand what he has to say. What you know for sure is that he's not making the contributions he should to these meetings. The company isn't getting the full benefit of his thinking.

What, then, is your move? Choose one.

> a) From now on, you tell him to pass along any ideas he has directly to you. You will then distribute them to the proper places yourself. And you add that you certainly hope he can come up with some suggestions more often.
>
> b) You call him in and tell him congratulations! He's been picked for that personality development course and is going to spend two weeks in Chicago taking it.
>
> c) You set up a highly selective planning group with just you, the research chief, and a couple of engineering types. You schedule bimonthly meetings and you're sure useful ideas will come out of them.
>
> d) You ask around and find out who in the company knows the research chief's inner thoughts better than anyone else. Who's his best friend, who really understands him? Then you work on him through this third party.

Choose your course of action and jot down your choice. Now go on to the other cases and do the same. We'll talk about my answers later.

CASE NUMBER 2: THE KID IN DEEP WATER

The new branch manager in Omaha is brilliant. He shows great promise and is going to be a crown prince one of these days, or so everybody says. But right now he lacks experience and it shows. What's more, your competitor is moving into the plains states with an intense marketing drive. The situation is growing tense. The marketing vice president confers with you because he knows you've taken a personal interest in the young branch manager's development. Should he pull him out temporarily and replace him with an older, surer hand? The vice president thinks so. What about you? After due consideration, you ...

a) Agree.
b) Agree, but give the man a special temporary assignment of some kind so that it won't look as though he's being brought back out of the line of fire.
c) Overrule the marketing vice president. Tell him the kid in Omaha will sink or swim.
d) Overrule him, but send a trouble-shooter or two out to Nebraska to help out during this crisis.

CASE NUMBER 3: THE LONER

Your international manager, a French-born U.S. citizen, is an implacable individualist. He's sure of his own judgment, frequently impatient with others, and darn near every time turns out to be right. There's that one problem, of course, that he's not much of a team player. Sometimes he ruffles the fur of his executive peers, and you know that most of this is needless in a man as sharp as he is. Now he's off on a new kick. He wants to open a plant in the north of Italy where he's sure the costs are going to work out fine. But there are several things about the project that don't add up in your mind. This time, in fact, you, the chief executive, are absolutely certain your international manager is wrong. However, you don't want to risk losing him because of his volatile judgment. Or do you?

a) Have him come to your country place for a weekend during which the entire economics of the whole thing are pored over. After all, you could be wrong yourself and if so, this lengthy study session will bring it to light. On the other hand, if you're as correct as you think, you should be able to convince him.
b) Quickly set up a special study committee to marshall the

facts and report to you (and to him) no later than two months.

c) Send this brilliant but restless chap one of those cryptic and generalized memos I mentioned earlier, so that he will look deeper into the situation on his own.

d) Seize the opportunity to present him with the largest challenge you can think of, some venturesome project you've been keeping in the back of your head about opening distribution in, say, Yugoslavia. And tell him, incidentally, to forget about the Italian plant.

CASE NUMBER 4: THE OLD PRO

Your vice president and controller is so thoroughly good at his job, so efficient, so reliable, and so experienced, that it's difficult to find fault with him. But Simon Legree that you are—you do. He just isn't making quite the seasoned contribution to the executive committee that you have a right to expect, in view of his accomplishments. He's too inclined to say things like, "If you are all determined to go ahead, then I'll go along with you. But I can tell you right now it's going to get us in trouble with people who look for earnings dilution." Instead of these sour jibes, he ought to be stating his case and fighting for it, so that the right decision can be hammered out. He's a superior executive and you want only the very best he has to offer. So how do you get him on the team again?

a) Set ironclad goals in all areas of his operations and see that he lives up to them.

b) See if you can get his juices running high by sending him to an advanced management course.

c) Assign one of those bright young men to be his assistant and give the youngster a lot of attention—until the old boy gets the message.

d) What about some of those cryptic memos of mine?

CASE NUMBER 5: THE CONSCIENTIOUS OBJECTOR

It's no secret to you that your top engineer is losing interest in his job. A crime, at his youthful age. But if your guess is right, it's because he misses the academic discipline and the action that once was so much a part of his life. He was a good man in the field, in the open air, and he misses it. He also figures he's losing his special skills and that all in all, the close air of the executive suite is stifling him. He's a gifted manager—but not unless you can keep his interest and spirit high. So?

a) Give him a big boost in salary and also try to lock him into the job, with deferred increments and bonuses.

b) Have a frank talk with him, and if he wants to get back out where he can actually build that bridge or lay that pipeline, then let him. All of us have only one life. But make sure it's with your company and not with somebody else.

c) Give the man a sabbatical to catch up on his professional credits, or travel, or whatever. Give him one every few years if necessary.

d) Tell the guy to shape up or ship out.

All right, those are some problems to ponder. While you're turning them over in your mind, let's go on to other things. I will offer my own answers later on. Meanwhile, I hope that what is to be discussed now will influence your own decisions in each case.

WHAT BUILDS FIRES UNDER WHO?

It all started back in the 1920's at a Chicago plant of Western Electric. The company called the place the Hawthorne plant, and today industrial psychologists still talk about the "Hawthorne effect."

If you recall, what the research team from Harvard did in the most famous of their series of experiments was announce that lighting intensity was to be changed, then increase it only for one "experimental" group of employees, leaving it the same for another "control" group. Puzzling then—just as it is to many people today—was the fact that production went up for *both* groups. Then the experimenters continued to tinker with the lighting and other factors like length of rest period, work days, and wage incentive formulas. Most of the time production continued to go up, even when the changes were apparently unfavorable—such as installing a longer work day.

The inescapable conclusion was that the employees identified with their groups and were happy to have attention paid them. They *thought* the lights were being brightened even if they weren't.

As I mentioned in Chapter 2, the science of motivation kept on developing new insights, and men like Dr. Frederick Herzberg have given us a fairly good idea of how to motivate different kinds of people. But another theory, that of Dr. A. H. Maslow of Brandeis University, is especially important when it comes to the best motivation for your key men. Back in 1954, Dr. Maslow said that there seems to be a hierarchy of needs for each human being. It begins with the basic physiological and safety needs, then goes on to social needs, esteem needs, and finally "the need for self-actualization." Simply put, most people give priority to the first need until it is satisfied, then go on up the scale.

In short, the person who has achieved safety (a decent income, say), and also has enjoyed society and the esteem of others must then go on to a sense of self-fulfillment, the highest need of all.

And that is one strong reason why there is this obvious trend toward a form of democracy in corporations. How else can each employee—let alone each manager—eventually gain that all-important sense of self-fulfillment in his work and in his life?

THE DEMOCRATIC BUSINESS ORGANIZATION— WHAT IS IT?

If self-actualization is the ultimate motivator, as I believe it is, it remains for you, the president, to see that each of your people gets a chance to reach that goal, and that they in turn see that each of their people get the same opportunity, and so on down the line.

How can this be done? Let me mention a very interesting little exercise that's sometimes used in basic management courses. You set up two teams of five or six men each. One is organized as a dictatorship—one of the men is in full charge. The other is structured as a democracy, with a head man who must basically get the consent of the others before making his decisions. Then the two teams are given a series of tasks—putting together mechanical puzzles, for example, or building construction toys—to see which team can do each job faster. And the results?

In very simple jobs that required little thought, just fast action, the dictatorship usually wins.

In more complicated jobs, with variables and complexities, the democracy usually triumphs.

What does this prove? If your company has some very simple goals and the way to reach them is immediately obvious to all, then you should run it like a dictator. Frankly, I can't imagine any company of any size in today's industry that could have goals that simple. Otherwise, you need the participation of your people.

Of course, many a company has been started and brought to bloom by a wizard of an entrepreneur who was able to combine the skills, knowledge and drive in his own person. You know the kind—a genius in his way who brooks little opposition and who can inspire his people to follow him blindly into battle. We still have some of these valuable fellows with us today, and long may they flourish. However, the usual thing that happens to their companies is that when the guiding genius retires, dies, or finally loses touch with the changing realities of the market place, then the company also expires. Generally it's acquired by a larger company that might have started in the same way many years back, but is now a team-oriented organization designed for growth and survival over the long run.

More and more companies are coming to realize that long-term strength implies democracy. In a recent book called *The Temporary Society* (Harper-Row, 1969) Warren Bennis and Philip Slater take a hard look at business organizations and conclude that the traditional bureaucratic structure—the pyramid with its well-defined chain of command—is on the way out. The reasons are that it can't come up with enough innovation for modern industrial needs; it doesn't promote enough interdisciplinary or task force problem-solving and decision-making; and most of all, it doesn't heed the growing needs of the new professional man, whose loyalty is more to himself, his family, and his career than to the company he happens to work for.

The theory goes right back to Maslow: "Before individuals can be fully human and 'self-actualized,' organizational systems have to be developed that can cultivate the growth of fully human persons."

The new democratic corporations, say the authors, will boast such features as a free flow of criticism and ideas up and down the ladder, a collaborative leadership style, consensus decisions, a flexible organizational chart, and more attention to conflicts between individual and corporate needs and objectives.

Sound like a revolution? Maybe, but I think that by and large these men and others who call for a permissive or democratic business environment are correct.

DEMOCRACY IN ACTION

In a company like North American Rockwell, with its basic partnership between space-age scientists and a tough-minded commercial organization, this new style of management is of paramount importance. One of our big objectives has been to harness exotic aerospace technology to meet earthly market opportunities—both to improve the quality of life on earth and to provide the company with new avenues of profitable enterprise. The best way to promote this exchange, we've found, is simply having people from different disciplines, different backgrounds, and different echelons in the company meet informally to talk things over and explore ideas.

Malcolm Barnum, our marketing vice president in the Commercial Products Group, put it this way in a recent magazine article: "From my point of view, the critical thing about the space program is not the end in itself—that is, getting a man on the moon —but rather the fact that the program stimulates the greatest scientific minds in our country in a way that could not be equaled by any other project. It generates new ideas, disciplines, and concepts that are going to give us our unlimited future right here on earth.

"However, it is up to marketing men to interest these minds in non-celestial problems. And we can do so if we will be dreamers, along with them."

We've set up elaborate procedures for bringing the scientists together with the commercial marketers, for transferring technology, and for identifying new business opportunities, reviewing them and launching new products. But the basic ingredient, Mac Barnum says, is "simple human contact." The result has been some pretty exciting new ideas in our many diverse areas of operation, including one complete systems study of our textile operations that pointed the way toward some truly fascinating possibilities for new kinds of equipment. Changing needs and fashions all around the world indicate that the entire textile industry may be in for an overhaul, and we hope to be in the forefront.

To do the initial study I mentioned, we brought in systems analysis talent fresh out of the space program. We aroused the enthusiasm of these scientists in a very real way, by letting them reveal to themselves the huge possibilities for applying their rarified knowledge and skills to the world we live in.

In my own way, I try to promote this sense of participation and collaboration and free flow of ideas right up and down the line in our company. There's nothing more important, in my opinion.

Mainly, I try to set an example in small, day-to-day matters. On company flights, for instance, I circulate among both executives and secretaries, pouring coffee and handing out buns, and making an occasional joke.

An executive's relationship with people should flow out of his natural instincts and personality, not from his title. The president or chairman who sets himself up as a tin god not only ruins any chance of rapport with his organization, but he also takes most of the fun out of his own job.

Letting your hair down can be great therapy, I've found. "Well, you lawyers certainly have a knack of ruining a good deal," I might say to our legal counsel. What I'm really saying, of course, is thanks for warning us about some pitfalls in a move we were about to make.

As far as I'm concerned, the greatest advantage of a more democratic style of leadership is that you inspire permanent self-confidence in your people. This is to be promoted at every opportunity. The other day, for instance, one of our managers came in waving a sheaf of back orders to tell me that in his considered opinion we needed a hasty expansion of one plant. As it happened, I'd already looked into the situation and decided on a different course of action.

But I didn't tell him so. Instead I talked conversationally and got him into a discussion of the different aspects of the situation—space availability, labor supply in the area, the need to have backup facilities.

"You know," he said thoughtfully, "I'm getting the feeling that we ought to put up another plant entirely in that district."

"Think so? Your idea may have merit," I said. "Why don't you follow through on it?"

Sure—that's what I planned to do all along. And I'm not trying to set myself up as some kind of mastermind or manipulator of men. I'm just saying that this manager will follow through with more enthusiasm, understanding, and pizazz than he would if I'd said, "No, I already thought of that, and it's a bad idea. Here's what we'll do instead. . . ."

Men are inspired to do their best when you give them self-fulfillment, by somehow making the goals of the company and the individual the same—or at least not incompatible.

On the other hand, inner fires can easily be extinguished by:

● Fear

Psychologists tell us that fear of losing a job is simply not an appreciable factor any more. But there is another kind of fear that can be healthful—the fear of not doing a good job. The free-wheeling executives of today and those down the ranks in a company want to do their best. That's what it's all about. But start threatening them economically and you're likely to be laughed at to your face.

● Gobbledygook

It's an age-old curse of corporations as well as governments. And it's still with us. Planners sit at executive sessions and solemnly talk about "geographic rollouts" instead of saying they want to penetrate a market; or "integrated autonomy" instead of "delegation." People are always having "ongoing critiques" and darn near every time somebody sneezes we get another "synergistic effect."

There's nothing wrong with having a little fun with this kind of phraseology, but make sure you don't take it seriously. If it starts creeping into your memos and speeches and conversation, it'll drive your clear-minded managers nuts.

● The wrong kind of competition

"The spirit of competition," says one well-known industrial psychologist, "can breed mediocrity instead of excellence." That's if it's used wrong. When several men are competing with energy, imagination, and a certain fearlessness, the result can be a moving, going company. But if they're competing merely to win the personal favor of some man or group of men with their human prejudices, the result can be stagnation. The key, of course, is to see that the competitors are being judged on their real achievements, measured in some way that is as nonsubjective as possible.

COACH OUTSIDERS, TOO

Let me add right here that a president is responsible for motivating people *outside* the company, too. Just a couple of examples:

One night in Washington, after a rough day of top-level negotiations, I got a call that represented really bad news. A company we were about to acquire had decided to sell off a major division to somebody else. There had been no hint of this during our negotiations and I was as angry as I'll ever get. I swore a little, grabbed the phone, and put through a call to the president. The other executives in the room with me looked a little pale, wondering if I were going to upset the whole thing with a show of temper.

But no, that's not the way to get things done. A good coach must be a good actor. By the time the man was on the wire, I was full of charm and pleasantries. Firmly but politely, I started the job of persuading him to back down on his decision. In ten minutes he had agreed.

An associate of mine calls this "the gentlemanly art of getting things done—our way." And it's true that persuasion is an art.

When you're heckled by a disgruntled stockholder at an annual meeting—and it happens to even the most successful of companies—don't "blow your cool." Answer each question courteously, patiently. Maybe after the meeting you'll want to chat with him a while. You'll end up making that stockholder a firm supporter. I recall doing that after one recent meeting. I sat for a half-hour straddled backwards on a chair giving him a full and complete answer to the question he had asked. I'm not sure, but I think I built a little confidence in that man.

Then there was the time when a certain supplier of ours was having some quality-control problems. As a big customer we were prepared to insist that they put in new procedures. We talked it over with them at great length and made specific suggestions, but they weren't convinced. Now, should we use muscle? I ruled against it. We backed off and gave them a chance to straighten out their own problems in their own way. Forcing them to accept our solutions would hardly form the basis for a satisfactory long-term relationship. On the other hand, if they didn't shape up we could swing to another supplier.

I'm happy to report that their quality control improved immediately. I still don't know what procedures they're using, and I don't want to know.

NOW FOR YOUR VERDICT

Let's see if you and I agree on some of the specifics of championship coaching. Remember those hypothetical case histories? Here are my answers:

1. The reluctant dragon

In my view, (a) makes our reticent researcher too much a special case, and would take up too much of your time. As for (b), sending him to a personality development course, that's not likely to be a real solution. Nothing against those courses, but our man's problem runs deeper and is basically organizational. I'll listen to your arguments for (d), working with him through a third party, but my best answer here is (c), setting up a select planning group in which your research man's valuable ideas would be more likely to emerge.

2. The kid in deep water

Your marketing vice president ought to be watched, because his recommendation (a) is almost guaranteed to wreck the young manager's career. As for (b), congratulations wouldn't fool many people, least of all the kid. On the other hand, (c), letting him sink or swim, could save him, but it also could ruin him. My choice is (d), leaving him on the hot seat but giving him plenty of help, probably including some outside consultants.

3. The loner

Maybe I tricked you on this one; if you chose (c), that generalized memo that I'm so fond of—then we don't agree this time. The reason is that this self-confident individualist is far too impatient to bother with cryptology. It's best to approach him through (d), by deliberately setting him the largest challenge you can think of. People like him operate that way. And they're awfully good to have around. In an article about how corporation presidents are developed, Cornell's Andrew Hacker said: ". . . the ascent . . . is frequently aided by a specific 'record' he has acquired, most usually by taking on a very tough assignment and doing well at it." As for the other answers, both (*a*) and (*b*) are acceptable strategies, but in my opinion they won't solve this problem in and of themselves.

4. The old pro

You guessed it. This time I'd use my magic memo (*d*) to get him to delve deeper. Maybe I'd say, "Dear Bob: Wasn't it Abe Lincoln who said 'He has a right to criticize who has a heart to help'?" And I'd let him know I appreciated it when he began to make more positive contributions. As for (*b*), you might want to have him take a course, but this is really another matter, without direct relation to the problem at hand. Both (*a*) and (*d*) seem to me de-motivators, particularly (*d*), undermining his authority by assigning the young assistant.

5. The conscientious objector

As I hope we've established in this chapter and others in this book, (*a*), palm greasing is not really a blaze-kindler these days by itself. Of course (*d*) is foolishness, the idea being to motivate, not dismiss your talented people, so that leaves (*b*), having the frank talk and letting him make a change in his career if he wants, or (*c*), offering sabbaticals. Now many companies have tried (*c*) in situations like this. It's a fine compromise—the only trouble with it is that it seldom works, not in a highly technical field. It takes more than part-time attention to keep up with a scientific or engineering discipline in this age. That leaves (*b*), and I think it's your only choice. Of course all these answers are arguable. Compare my answers with yours. Talk them over with other people. That's the route to managerial wisdom.

Before removing our Coach's Cap, let's look at a few special kinds of individuals. As a corporation president, you'll meet these over and over again. How do you get them to do their best?

THE HIGH ACHIEVER

He's like the bright kid in school—he may get bored if operations move at a pace that accommodates the duller average youngsters. Your job in keeping him fired up is to continually confront him with challenges. Vincent McGuinness of Shareholders Management Company says it's a matter of keeping a man just below his "comfort zone." In other words, never let him slip into a feeling of self-satisfaction with his job, his income, his production. That's as good a way of putting it as any. Keep raising the level of your expectations.

And don't think this contradicts the ideal of "self-actualization." Part of life's satisfaction—a large part of it—is in the striving.

THE MIND-CHANGER

Ever close a meeting with the certainty that everybody had agreed, only to find out later that at least one of the agreers actually had definite reservations and, in fact, is now stalling the project? Well, you could always call him up and tell him to get moving or else, but there are other and better ways.

First, make sure that everybody *does* agree. Beware of letting your own enthusiasm convince you that everyone was going along with your ideas, when actually they were just tired of arguing.

Still, there may be a chronic mind-changer and eventually you've got to get his cooperation. My suggestion is to avoid pressing him for agreement during the meeting. The reason he seems to change his mind later is probably that he needs to think about the problem in private. Maybe he doesn't function too well in groups. So tell him he can have a certain period of time to enter his objections, if any—but after that insist on a firm opinion—in writing.

THE OUTSIDER

He's not very social, contributes little to group meetings, almost never gets together with his peers to bat around ideas. Yet he's a useful man and you'd like to get more out of him, both for his own sake and for the company's. What approach do you take? I'd say you should accept his "outsiderness" and take advantage of it.

Use him as a sounding board, almost as you would a third-party consultant. He's detached and he'll speak his mind—if you ask him. And don't rule out his participation in groups. His "man from Mars" objectivity may be just what you need to reconcile differences in an executive group.

THE TEMPORARY FAILURE

Having fumbled a big assignment, he feels that his career is over. He's in a state of shock, but you realize he has better things ahead and want to bring him out of his depression—and quick. The first thing you must do is get things clear in his mind on exactly what happened. Make sure he knows what went wrong— and also what parts of the operation he did right. Show how others should share the blame—including you if you gave him an assignment he wasn't ready for.

The last time I was involved in a situation like this I said to the youthful manager in question:

> Spending that kind of money without testing the market more carefully was a pretty bad mistake, all right. It's costing us. I won't deny it. I also won't deny that I knew what was happening and didn't stop you. So let's put the thing in perspective. Messing up a job is one thing. How you feel about it is another. If you let this thing get to you, then it will be a lot more costly to us both than it has been so far.

We gave him an assignment of comparable importance just a few weeks later. And he came out charging.

One final word about you and your Coach's Cap. Listen to the words of Vince Lombardi greeting a new team member in his film, *Second Effort:*

> Football is a spartan game with its qualities of sacrifice and self-denial. It's a game of violent contact. Because of that violent contact, there's a personal discipline required that is seldom found in any other place in this modern world. We're going to ask you to work harder than you've ever worked before . . .

And now listen to lineman Jerry Kramer, speaking of his former mentor:

> He inspires confidence, and drives himself harder than he drives his team. I've never met anybody like him, and I can tell you that the things he believes in really work.

Your job is nothing less than to inspire the same sentiments in those who toil for you.

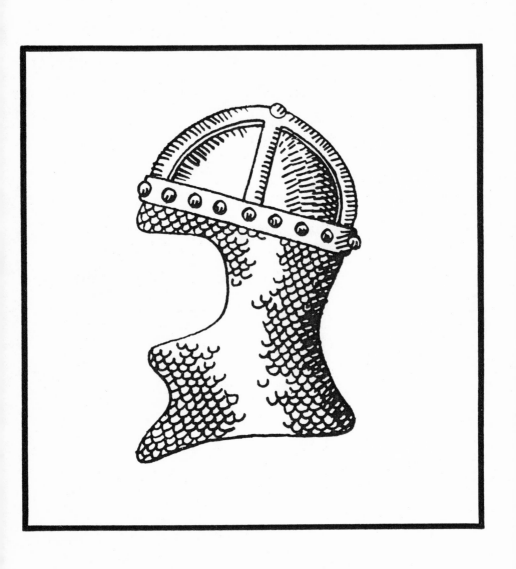

CHAPTER TEN

The Hat of the Crusader

"There is a certain blend of courage, integrity, character and principle which has no satisfactory dictionary name," wrote Louis Adamic, "but has been called different things at different times in different countries. Our American name for it is 'guts.'"

And guts is what American industry keeps saying it wants in its executives, its managers and supervisors. It's almost as if we see ourselves donning armor every day, taking spear and shield in hand and riding off to fight the Infidel. The image is only slightly exaggerated. Listen, for instance, to this message recently delivered by one executive to a group of management trainees at a big company in the east:

> I want men who're not afraid to fight me for what they believe is right for the company and for themselves. I want men who aren't scared to make decisions that might cost the company some money and, yes, might cost them their jobs if they're wrong. I want guys who're willing to lay their jobs on the line every day.

Was he kidding, do you think? Is it realistic to expect your people to repeatedly risk their livelihoods, to come to the office each morning full of daring, death-defying projects?

I'd say this particular executive was laying it on too thick. Locked inside the Helmet of the Crusader, he lost sight of some of the elementary rules of human behavior. It's my belief that risks can and must be taken on every level of business, but not just to be a hero or because of some inner call to arms. History tells us that Richard the Lion-Hearted was neither an effective monarch nor an especially successful crusader.

At North American Rockwell we try to do our jousting in a steadier, less flamboyant way. Business risks—which are what we are basically discussing in this chapter—should be a natural, normal, almost inevitable part of every manager's operation. I mean sound, reasoned risks—the kind you go into with your eyes very wide open. And it's still another of the president's many jobs to create an atmosphere so that all his people are willing and able to ante up in an intelligent way.

You won't create this atmosphere by running your department like a riverboat gambler. If you always seem to be playing for desperately high stakes, and depending on luck, this will undermine your people's confidence in you. Nor should you run the shop like a caricature of a Marine field commander, shouting "Gung ho" as you lead your men to certain death. Business units, like armies, can be kept keyed up and combat ready just so long.

No, your job is to make it *easy and natural* for your people to take the ordinary risks that go with the competitive realities of industry—and also, on occasion, some of the not so ordinary ones. For instance, you want your managers to:

—approve outlays of cash within their province without quaking in their boots or running to you for every decision;

—take a chance on promising subordinates who need testing under fire;

—be able, in marketing, to take bold steps involving unusual advertising campaigns and the like;

—get out of their ruts and think of new and perhaps better ways to accomplish their unit goals;

—take a stand against their peers and also their superiors, including you, if the question and their convictions are crucial enough.

And, of course, there's much more. And all of it starts with one ingredient—their confidence in you, the ultimate boss, the chief executive. You must be able to take your own risks—which of course are much greater in scope than anyone else's—and you must get your managers to do as you do. Step one, I'd say, is an understanding of just what a risk is in business. Often it looks a little riskier than it really is. It helps to get rid of the demonology. What, after all, is a "bold businessman"?

Here are a few examples:

The bold recruiter

"Humdrum job got you headed for hippieland?" inquired an ad that appeared in eastern newspapers not long ago. "Don't drop out—drop in!" That was just a sample of the bright appeals to bright youth launched by the company, United Nuclear Corporation of White Plains, New York. A few others:

"Before you try flower power, give a thought to nuclear power."
"Intelligent aliens and qualified humanoids are welcome at United Nuclear—we pay relocation costs."
"Is there intelligent life at United Nuclear?"

Sure, it was a little risky. No one else had ever tried to recruit young scientists and technical people that way. But United Nuclear had the notion that the people it wanted were not the soberside types so often pictured, but a highly creative and unconventional breed. Apparently they were right. The campaign drew 50 percent more replies than previous efforts and a good percentage of them were fine prospects.

Some companies are reported to be going even further. They're even considering sending recruiters out on the college circuit in long hair, steel-rim glasses, and desert boots, to tell students things like: "I hear you think a career in financial management may be your bag. Well, we have a training program at our company that will really blow your mind." Another suggested recruiting ad:

> If you want to take the conventional, easy way out, and you only want to feel good all over, then you'd better join the Peace Corps. But if you want to work hard for low pay, doing work that is sometimes boring and even dangerous— just look at the incidence of alcoholism and neurosis in American business—then our company may be the spot for you.

Approaches like this, of course, are sometimes successful, sometimes not. But they illustrate a basic point about bold businessmanship. Chances are taken with a clear purpose in mind—and often because the conventional approach hasn't worked.

There's a lot more to risky recruiting. Did you know that a large number of companies have had excellent results for years in hiring ex-convicts—and even current prisoners on work-release programs who must return under lock and key at nights? Such companies, to avoid embarrassing their employees, never publicize these programs.

But they get good, loyal people, by and large. And they reduce their risks considerably through a system of keeping in close touch with wardens, parole officers, and clergymen to find likely prospects.

The bold marketer

"Dear Mr. Brown: You are not doing your job," a West Coast sales manager once wrote to the head buyer of a major department store. "You're supposed to see every salesman in your field at least once. It's your duty and your obligation. But our man has been calling for six months and you won't give him the time of day. I find this inexcusable."

This sales manager had a boss who in turn had a boss—the company president—who didn't believe in knuckling under to customers or prospects who didn't play fairly. In this case the account seemed completely out of reach so the sales manager decided to take a drastic stand, which would at least get the buyer's attention. Not to his surprise, the buyer realized his error, made an appointment with the salesman, and eventually became a customer.

The whole thing was actually less risky than it might seem, but just the same, the sales manager and the company rightfully earned a reputation for individualism, self-confidence, and flair. It's a good reputation for any company to have, and the attitude must start at the top.

Back in 1946, Emery Air Freight Corporation, newly formed, thought it had a good idea for a useful service to business and public. But it wasn't getting anywhere against giant Air Express until it got the benefit of (1) a piece of luck—Air Express went on strike; and (2) a bold investment of time and money. What happened was that the Federal Reserve Bank was looking for a company to study its entire system of moving bags of checks. With Air Express out of the running, little Emery decided to bet some time and money on the experimental venture. It came up with not only a marketing program for this one customer but also a system for marketing its services to all customers—a system that has since made it one of the interesting success stories of postwar industry.

If a bold marketing stance is evident at the top level of a company, the philosophy will flow right down through the ranks and, incidentally, will result in better men in the field. The company will be less likely to use the stodgy screening and testing procedures that, in the words of the marketing psychologist Dr. Herbert Greenberg, "leave out the creative thinker, the free spirit, the original, imaginative and hard-driving individual who often makes the best salesman."

Many companies are careful to avoid that mistake. A graphic arts company, for instance, according to its sales vice president, culls out any "real beatniks," but beyond that, looks for individualism. "Salesmen are different from cost accountants or anybody else who comes into the same snug harbor every day," he says. "So we evaluate their performance carefully after we hire them, insist that they meet quotas and provide full coverage of the territory and keep their managers informed of their itinerary. But as to exactly how they meet their goals—we leave them pretty much on their own."

The way I see it, the president who isn't looking for a snug harbor can create an entire company in his own venturesome image, especially in the marketing area.

The bold organizer

At North American Rockwell, one wit remarked, sometimes you can't tell the managers from the office boys without a program. The reason is that a lot of departments are headed up by young men we were willing to take a chance on. They showed evidence of being able to handle more responsible jobs, so they got them.

Some people say we're taking too much of a chance with inexperienced hands at these helms. They said the same thing back in 1964, when I moved to Rockwell-Standard and left Rockwell Manufacturing in the hands of Clark Daugherty as president. He was aggressive, sure, the critics admitted, but at 40, how could he cope with the complexities of a company that had made 22 acquisitions in 15 years? Well, he coped. He got results. The doubters were wrong then, and I believe they're wrong now.

But risk-taking in organizational matters means a great deal more than gambling on young talent. It also means gambling on *old* talent, when the situation calls for it, and it means at every turn organizing a division or department or a whole company along lines that give a man the chance to excel, rather than plod along safely.

Sentry Insurance Company, a few years ago, threw out its old pyramid organization chart and made up a new one consisting of "circles" of people. The idea was to emphasize participative management and give each key employee functions apart from his primary job.

That was the answer to their particular problem. Other companies try other innovations, setting up the kind of organization that works for them in the finest and best way, instead of the kind of organization they find in textbooks. About five years ago, we re-cast Rockwell-Standard along the lines of what one magazine called "controlled decentralization." Though each division retained its independence, at the same time individual plant managers were made accountable for profits on both short and long-term bases.

Another case in point is Wells, Rich, Greene, an advertising agency that in only a few years of operation has become one of the best-known of the creative shops. It has a unique organizational setup—one of the smallest staffs in the business in relation to the size of its billings. Other agencies with comparable volume have more than twice the number of people working for them. But Mary Wells Lawrence, the president, believes in hiring expensive, executive-level people and then having *them* do the actual work. And she won't hire recent graduates, or at least very few, declining to run a "training school." Another organizational maverick, and it works for them.

Challenge your own chart! See that it serves your special purposes, instead of vice versa.

The bold manager

And this, of course, is what it all comes down to. The truly successful manager must know how to take sensible risks in every facet of his operation. Bert S. Cross, chairman of Minnesota Mining and Manufacturing, keeps a miniature golden turtle on his desk. "This fellow," he would say, "knows he can't make any progress unless he sticks his neck out."

What is the daring manager really like? Here are some of his identifying traits:

1. *Sometimes he plays hunches . . . at least, they seem to be hunches.*

How is it that he seems to know things about the market—what some of its needs are going to be a few years from now, which products are going to move toward obsolescence and which toward greater acceptance? How does he seem to know so much about other companies—who the real power is when it comes to engineering specs, who's going to succeed to top management, who will emerge as the chief after a merger shakeup? How does he know which of his people will prove out, which lines will expand, what the government is going to do?

No manager, of course, can know all these things. But as pointed out in Chapter 3, the adroit manager knows how to have a pretty solid hunch about them. As I mentioned at that time, it's not a hunch at all but a carefully thought-out estimate of the probabilities, based on massive research. That's how to wear the Hat of the Soothsayer. And to wear the Hat of the Crusader, you must *take action* on these hunches or "funny feelings." You must have the courage of your conjectures.

So see what information you've got in the back of your head, or the back of the file—and bring it out.

2. *He asks for trouble . . . but that doesn't mean he gets it.*

When he's addressing a company gathering, be it a group of recruits or the board of directors, the bold manager tells them what's wrong with the company and its programs as well as what's right. He discusses problems frankly and sometimes remarks, "I may as well tell you that this project of ours is going to fall flat on its face—unless each and every one of you gets behind it with all your strength."

He holds neither products nor services in sacred awe. "I don't dispute that we've been making money on this item for the past 30 years," he might say. But this is history. Tomorrow the product will have to be modified if we are to compete successfully." Regardless of the area, the daring manager rarely wants for problems to "go away."

3. *He gets his people to stick their necks out . . . by sticking out his own.*

For one thing, he does it in the small ways. If he wants a particular goal met, he offers real and valuable incentives. And he sticks his neck out in the large ways, too, going to bat for a man who may have made a wrong decision that cost the company money, but who is worth saving. He risks championing unpopular causes within and without the company. He does battle, if he must, with suppliers, government agencies, unfair competitors.

I recall the case of a small company in the drug field. The packaging they ordered for one new product turned out badly. It was defective, and the resulting confusion in the marketplace caused the company financial loss. The package supplier, a giant corporation, offered a small settlement, but the president of the company turned it down flat and demanded a much larger one. He eventually took his case to the packaging chairman of the board, running the risk of getting nothing at all. But he persuaded the chairman he'd been unfairly treated and his demands were met in full.

This kind of bold approach does not go unnoticed by the people who work for the Crusader. It sets the best kind of example.

4. *He breaks the rules . . . but not just for the fun of it.*

In an emergency, the daring manager will cheerfully break the most cherished rule he himself ever made. He'll take it upon himself to change specifications, approve a financial matter and the like, if there isn't time to use established procedure. But then he may re-establish the rule, or alter and restate it if he thinks there will be more exceptions. And he'll explain the entire episode to everyone who would have been involved under the procedure temporarily set aside.

5. *He argues with success . . . and often wins.*

The mere fact that a system is working doesn't mean he's sold on it. Maybe there's still another way of doing it faster, cheaper, or more reliably. Maybe a different method will stand up better as times and industries change. And he brings his subordinates in on the process. He calls in the marketing chief and says, "I've just had a crazy idea. What if we changed the label on the product and sold it to teenagers instead of adults? Would we gain more customers than we'd lose in the next ten years?" Or in another line, "What if we converted the Speedfill so it would work with those new plastic bottles? Would we get into some new markets at our price?"

Some psychologists call it "lateral thinking." One consulting firm, Dunlap and Associates, calls in "Neologics" (new logic). What it means is freeing the mind from convention so that it can take the kind of flights that might lead to a rainbow, complete with pot of gold.

6. *He says what's on his mind . . . and somehow people like him for it.*

Not long ago one company headed by an acquaintance of mine lost out in a highly important decision by a government agency. The reason they lost the decision was that they wouldn't fight for it, and the reason they wouldn't fight for it was that they were afraid of becoming controversial.

The company had another unrelated public relations problem and had been getting some unfavorable publicity—mostly unjustified, but there it was. Now they would do anything to keep their name out of the papers, even give in to what was really an unfair decision by the agency.

I say they were too cautious. A company, like a man, must speak its mind.

This applies right down the line. If a subordinate makes a bad mistake, for example, you don't do him a service by trying to minimize it. Tell him what he did wrong. If you're a good manager in other ways he'll know what you're telling him is just, and that you're doing it for his sake as well as the company's.

It's all in the way that you do it. In politics, for instance, you can disagree with somebody without making him an enemy for life. Voters are always being surprised to learn that some Senators who seldom agree on the floor are actually personal friends. And in business dealings, you can fight hard for your position without making enemies. All it takes is respect for the other person.

And, perhaps, a little humor. The marketing force for one company was under strict instructions not to "knock" a competitive company that kept imitating its products, but they were told they could refer to the other outfit as "Me Too, Inc."

7. *Finally, he's not afraid to change his mind . . . because he doesn't believe in beating a dead horse.*

It's the final risk. When you know you're wrong, you rise above your emotions and remind yourself that no one really thinks you're infallible, anyway. So you explain your reasons and announce your change of mind—without being apologetic about it either.

THE COMPANY YOU'RE IN

Virtually, all of America's great industrialists have worn the Hat of the Crusader, but some more than others. Here are some of the great ones:

Joseph Wilson and his associates took a gamble that the recognized surveys were wrong, and that business actually could find a use for extra copies of its documents and would pay for a quick way to get them. Or, as we say nowadays, no matter what brand of copier we're actually using, "to Xerox them."

George Romney gambled that the public at the turn of the last decade was ready for a compact car, and for the time being, at least, he was 100 percent right.

And going way back in that industry, *Henry Ford* staked everything on the quaint notion that American families would buy a cheap, reliable motor car—painted black.

Thomas Watson, Jr., bet on the idea that these strange new devices called computers were not just rarefied gadgets to be used only by universities and scientists, but would become a business tool of unparalleled power—and that a company called IBM could lead the way.

John T. Connor decided that although drugs had been a traditionally profitable industry, the record could be improved upon by assembling an outstanding research staff and spending unprecedented sums in that area. As a result, Merck & Company now gets upwards of three-quarters of its sales from products introduced within the last ten years.

Not all the great risk-takers head giant corporations. *Jeno F. Paulucci* gambled everything on the obviously absurd idea that an Italian could make exotic Chinese food in an out-of-the-way place like Duluth, Minnesota, and sell it profitably all over the nation. The result was the Chun King Corporation, an outstanding success in specialty foods.

In our own way at North American Rockwell we like to think of ourselves as courageous. For instance, *Lee Atwood and I* gambled that it is indeed possible to profitably combine aerospace and commercial industrial markets, taking the best from both worlds and making one benefit from the other. So far it would appear that our gamble is paying off.

All these men were willing to go on their intuition, their hunches, their creativity or whatever you might call that mysterious force. But none of them, not one, relied on that alone. They all amassed great amounts of information before making their critical decisions. And that's what you must do to make your own gambles pay off.

FACTS, FACTS AND MORE FACTS

The Crusader who relies too much on intuition is sure to get unhorsed by the first Saracen who comes along. You simply cannot take rational risks without an information system of the first rank.

Elsewhere in this book I have discussed how a company president can arrange to have information flow to him from all the eyes and ears of the company and from a lot of other places as well, including the seats of government. But it's equally important that this information—the right amount of it and no more—continue its flow to key individuals in your organization. There must be a smooth passage of great masses of usable facts up and down the line, if you are to have a basis for the chances you must take, and if each of your people is to have enough to go on so that he can perform the vital service of sticking his own neck out.

Now, how is this done? It's a whole science in itself, one that is constantly being improved upon as new technology and new ideas are brought forth by those methodical maniacs for order, the system specialists. You don't have to be one yourself, but you must understand how they work and you must know when you need one.

The breakdowns in information reporting can amaze you. Recently the head man at a company in Ohio was wondering just what could be going wrong at his main plant. Shipments were late, frequently in error. Profits were a mess. Call a meeting of the six key men at the plant and you'd get six different and very strident opinions of what the trouble was. So the president sighed and called in a systems consultant who spent three months quietly interviewing dozens of people on all levels of management and supervision.

"We were getting sick and tired of waiting," the president said, "and figured we had wasted the money and were still up against it. And then this systems man comes and tells me that he had re-designed all our forms and was ready to give me a complete new information-reporting system including just who would get what form and what he would do with it and a million other things—all computerized.

"By the time he finished explaining it to me I was darned near bowled over. But it made sense and we have the most efficient operation in our industry now.

"Incidentally, he found out the immediate cause of our shipments problem. The foreman of one department had a temperamental problem and had demoralized his crew. That one little thing had sent out waves of trouble in ever-increasing circles all over the plant. Our new system keeps this from happening anywhere."

Of course, you shouldn't be surprised by a report as this president was. The more usual procedure is for you, the chief executive, to be kept informed at every step of the way, and to be given preliminary reports in some detail at various stages. However it comes about, though, many a company has greatly improved its risk-taking capabilities by getting a firm foundation of facts routinely, every day of operation.

One small Connecticut company had high inventory costs and didn't know why. The consultants they brought in found that the problem was traceable to sales forecasting. This operation had been hit or miss, based on unreliable and out-of-date presumptions, and as a result the production people just didn't know how much of any one item would be needed in a given period. A sophisticated computerized sales forecasting system, designed by the consultants, solved that particular problem and some other unsuspected problems as well. With this information in hand daily, the president of the company embarked on a bold diversification plan. He was able to take some risks because at last he had a reliable idea of what his bread-and-butter business would be like for any period of the year.

In any company, in any field, there's no substitute for information. TRW, the technology-oriented conglomerate that has managed to avoid many of the problems of similar companies, relies on an intensive monthly reporting system. Each of its 50 operating areas is a separate profit center, and most produce a full profit-and-loss statement and balance sheet within five days of the end of each month. The system at the moment is being computerized to provide TRW's top management with the information it needs to take its own risks and to keep a rein on the risks of each of the 50 managers.

A good system of information, then, must:

—report the essential facts to each individual, and no more;

—limit itself to controllable items;

—be easy to understand and apply;

—provide for frequent reports at the lower levels, less frequent ones at the higher levels;

—facilitate comparison of results to plans and standards;

—cover only facts that have something to do with end results of the company or unit—no facts for facts' sake.

HOW TO TAKE CHANCES

Assuming, now, that you do have this solid base of information, and that you understand some of the characteristics of the mentality of the successful Crusader, let's get down to brass tacks. What follows is a suggested procedure for taking a risk.

First, go into the venture with your eyes wide open. Don't kid yourself that what you're doing is "the only thing to do under the circumstances." There are *always* options. Examine them all before deciding on *any* course, risky or super-safe.

Second, don't be afraid to use outside help. "When we discuss our service with Mr. President," a Houston management consultant told me recently, "we are dealing with a human being who has an ego and is reluctant to say, 'Yes, we need your help.' Or if he does admit it, we are confronted by his staff who may feel differently." Before laying a substantial amount of company cash on the line, you as president should get the best opinion and advice you can find.

Third, keep your cool. The pilot of an airplane doesn't call the stewardesses into the cockpit to say, "Wow, there's a terrible thunderstorm down there!" Nor should you let even your closest associates know about your little doubts or fears as the game proceeds. That's the loneliness of the commander. If you seem to have second thoughts about risks, so will everyone who works for you, resulting in general over-cautiousness. Above all, you must inspire confidence.

Fourth, go all out. Play the game as if you had no alternative, which brings us to the next point.

Fifth, know what you will do if the plan fails. Except in extremely rare emergencies, you should have your plans all ready to go into action if your gamble fails, or doesn't prove to be quite as successful as you hoped. Even though you *act* as if everything depends on the success of the risk, you make sure that everything does *not* depend on it.

Sixth, don't let a temporary setback cool your ardor for sensible risk-taking. Remember Bert Cross's turtle. If he stopped sticking his neck out everytime he met an obstacle, he would shortly die inside his shell.

When L. F. McCollum was chairman of Continental Oil Co., he put it this way:

> Too often the proprietary system of yesteryear frustrated imagination and creativeness. Talented comers were frequently supressed. Today the prospects are brighter . . . the premium now is where it should have been years ago— on ingenuity, imagination, aggressiveness, creative drive, and on individual contribution. We are in the midst of a knowledge explosion unprecedented in the history of mankind. Our challenge is not just to *cope* with it, but to contribute to it. *To initiate change.* To innovate, and *keep innovating.*

Once all that is said, however, there remains the practical problem I referred to at the beginning of the chapter. How long can you keep that exciting go-go atmosphere alive in your company, without beginning to bore your people? There must be a balance. Sometimes there must be routine, even dull days. There must be variations, changes of pattern. No one job or one life can be all the same—not even all enthusiasm and excitement.

There is perhaps a more personal question here. How long can you yourself go on managing a vast complex of things and people, go on taking these chances that must be taken in business —and still stay on an even keel?

The very young executive doesn't think about this, nor should he. But recent reports from industrial and business psychologists report that the outlook from some executive suites is increasingly neurotic and despondent. For executives involved in mergers, for example, who are suddenly confronted with younger and perhaps better-educated and certainly more aggressive rivals, this is a severe crisis. According to *Dun's Review*, the executive of a large corporation, once "the most secure of men," now is almost the only professional man or worker who has no protection. Since so many executives live slightly beyond their means —no matter how large the means—they stand in peril of sudden financial disaster in a day of free-wheeling company swallow-ups and massive reorganization.

Many companies such as Eastman Kodak, IBM, and DuPont have set up in-house psychiatric facilities to deal with the tensions of all their employees. And others have shown a new willingness to hire or re-hire executives who have recovered from mental crackups. "They've learned that people don't come poured out of a cement mold, and they judge on performance instead of personality," one psychiatrist commented.

This still leaves a great burden, however, on you—the man at the top. It is perhaps the greatest risk of the Corporate Crusader.

The ultimate boss has some releases, it is true. As Dr. Mortimer Feinberg has said, "The top executive has a big playpen and more toys on which to work out his neuroses than, say, the poor truckdriver who can only bang himself around at home. The president of one company I know, for example, has a grandiosity hang-up. He always insists that the elevator be cleared out so that he can ride up to his office alone."

But once these grand toys are taken away, the top man will fall farther and harder than anyone else. And of course those who indulge in them are showing these symptoms. My advice, for what it's worth, is this:

Don't consider yourself infallible. You aren't. Don't expect to succeed in every risk. You won't. Keep a sense of humor about your work, your company and most of all, yourself. This won't keep you from ever getting "uptight" but it will help you to cope with it when it happens.

THE PRIZE IS TO THE BOLD

Let me close by recounting one of the best examples I know of in the annals of corporate risk-taking. What Eastern Air Lines did in 1964 and 1965 under the leadership of its new president, Floyd D. Hall, is perhaps the classic case of the bold industrial "turnaround."

From 1960 to 1963, Eastern had lost a total of almost $60 million. Its equipment was old; its service was in disrepute. Some regular travelers on its routes even formed a club called WHEALS, Inc., which meant We Hate Eastern Air Lines. But the new management team took strong hold, secured emergency financing, and started the risky road to recovery. Instead of conservatively trying to make do with what it had and hope for gradual recovery, the airline invested heavily in new equipment from jets to electronic reservation systems to new uniforms for stewardesses.

Boldest of all, perhaps, Eastern talked openly about its past troubles as a way of calling attention to its new spirit. The company produced a film, "Sunrise at Eastern," which told the story of the bleak past and the brightening future. The film was shown to all employees and to the press and other outsiders. This bold honesty paid off. Soon employees were forming committees in various cities to push company sales.

In January, 1965, Eastern unveiled a new "corporate identity" built around new symbols and markings for its planes and all equipment, new approaches to advertising and the entire spectrum of communications. More new jets were ordered. New terminals and office buildings were put up in key markets around the country, and computerized activities were expanded to flight planning and maintenance.

Eastern went from tenth to first place in on-time operations among major airlines in one period. It cut its losses to $5.8 million in 1964 and then, at the end of 1965, turned its first profit since 1959—about $28.5 million.

Were Eastern's troubles all over, like the sudden passing of a Caribbean thunderstorm? Hardly. Show me a company whose troubles are over for good and I'll show you a company that has just been merged out of existence. No, Eastern still has its good and bad periods, just as all of us do. But in those two years it pulled itself up from the depths to a relatively secure position in its industry. This was all done through good, sound business practices—an inseparable part of which were reasoned risks in the areas of finance, operations, marketing, and public relations.

If you can come up with the same mix, on any scale, you're on your way to understanding the responsibilities of the president's office.

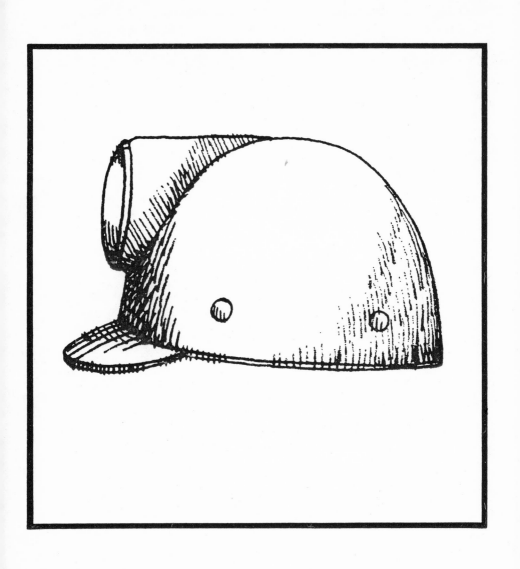

CHAPTER ELEVEN

The Hat of the Miner

WHAT SHOULD WE AND COULD WE BE DOING THAT WE ARE NOT DOING?

This is a question that nags—or should nag—at a chief executive night and day, seven days a week and fifty-two weeks a year.

Are we tapping all profit mines to the hilt? Are we digging deeply enough? Are we using the proper tools of excavation?

The dynamic, forward-moving industrial organization does not take profit exploitation for granted. Nor does it dig at random and by chance. At North American Rockwell, for example, we believe that the subject merits number one priority above all other corporate considerations. Profit exploitation is thoughtfully structured and carefully pre-planned. Since we are essentially a technologically oriented company, the vitally important area of getting every last ounce of profit out of our technology will serve as a prime example to illustrate what is involved in the systematic and comprehensive trackdown of profit opportunities.

GET THE WHEELS TURNING AND KEEP THEM IN MOTION

I know one company where the president is properly concerned about progress and growth. Once each month he calls a meeting of the executive committee for the specific purpose of discussing opportunities and taking action to cash in on them.

This system is better than ignoring the problem altogether. Interesting ideas are discussed at the meetings. Decisions are made. Actions are taken.

But the system falls far short of what is needed to exploit profit opportunities to the hilt. For one thing, in an organization of hundreds, only a small handful of men participate in the mining activity on any concentrated or comprehensive basis. For another thing, experience has taught us that profit exploitations, to work with maximum effectiveness, must be not an occasional exercise but an everyday process. In short, all of the company's creative resources should be poured into the effort. And the mining operation should run round the clock.

From what I have seen, the companies that exploit profit opportunities most successfully are the ones that build the following four ingredients into their exploitation programs:

1. The never-ending, never-diminishing grow-mindedness of the chief executive.
2. The venture capital needed to back up ideas and inspiration the moment it is needed.
3. The organizational machinery that will carry investigation forward into all possible avenues of exploitation.
4. The whole-hearted participation and cooperation of talented people.

As in all fields of business and human endeavor, it is my conviction that ingredient number four is the most important one of all. The trick is to set those human wheels in motion and to keep them moving. That is where the planning and organization come in.

At North American Rockwell we have formed what we refer to as a Technology Exploitation Committee. It functions in a purely advisory capacity to corporate and group presidents. Serving on the committee are key members of management, engineering, production, and marketing—all the elements that are needed for a complete management decision. One of the committee's main tasks is communication. When minds don't meet, experience proves, exploitation in general and technological exploitation in particular, most frequently tends to break down. As the chairman of the Technology Exploitation Committee puts it: "Getting men of diverse disciplines to sing from the same sheet of music can be one hell of a challenge." That's why a major objective of the committee is to keep profit opportunities from getting sidetracked into semantic potholes.

Another goal is to trigger and sustain an interchange of ideas at the various divisional levels. The first step is identification. Exploitation usually begins with the identification of product needs and technical requirements. And it follows through with the identification of inventions and innovations. In a diverse, merger-minded organization corporate-wide identification geared to profit exploitation takes on a very special importance. As I stated in a *Harvard Business Review* article (Sept.-Oct. 1968 issue), in referring to the 1967 merger of Rockwell-Standard and North American Aviation, making a merger work is largely "a matter of meshing your resources into the resources of the other company and coming up with a whole that is greater than the sum of the parts—the well-known synergistic formula."

The problem is that it takes more than pep talks to achieve this end. It takes organized effort backed by well-oiled corporate machinery, sufficiently motivated individuals, and hard cash to generate a desired interchange of ideas on all levels and to break down the divisional barriers which tend to build up in most companies.

The payoff if you can pull this off is limited only by the imaginations of your people. Our recently developed "Straight Stop Brake" is a good example. The brake was invented in our Commercial Products Group. Its purpose is to prevent the jackknifing of cargo trailer trucks. Pilots of the brake were built and tested, but we were reluctant to release the product. We wanted an assurance of safety performance that was beyond the pale of ordinary testing. Where could we get such assurance? One place only—so the Technology Exploitation Committee decided to bring our Autonetics Division into the picture. Autonetics, as you may know, is the most technology-advanced discipline of its kind in the world. Our technical people in Anaheim, California, supplemented the commercial group's efforts with studies and tests of their own. When their final endorsement came through, it served to dissipate any lingering traces of doubt. Our long-range profit plans could proceed.

The point, however, is this. Divisional interchange of this kind does not happen automatically. The president has to *make* it happen. It is up to him to see to it that the proper corporate machinery—and personal motivation—are built into the program so that wide-ranging interaction cannot help but occur.

One further deterrent to profit growth is worthy of mention. That is the frequent need to bridge the gap between the inventor's zeal and the marketer's salesmindedness. Or the marketer's zeal and the engineer's hard-headed pragmatism. As the chairman puts it, "The factor least understood by many would-be technological exploiters is the essential need for compatibility between technical and marketing people."

Commercially, new technology has no value unless it adds to a marketability. And projected market specifications have no value if, like "perpetual motion," they cannot be made compatible with technology. Thus a final vital function of the Technology Exploitation Committee is the correlation of technical and marketing specifications. Without aggressive correlation and a resolute smoothing of the way, the entire exploitation effort is likely to bog down. All of the diverse factors and elements involved in the exploration and exploitation of ideas must be brought into proper focus like stereopticon pictures, if they are to be commercially effective.

GROW TENTACLES

The German poet Heinrich Heine once wrote, "Mark this well, ye proud men of action! Ye are, after all, nothing but unconscious instruments of the men of thought."

I can tell you this. Heine's "men of thought" have stood me in remarkably good stead in donning the Hat of the Miner. What it boils down to is a simple matter of multiplication. In mining, as in drilling for oil, the more holes you sink, the more rich veins you are likely to tap.

The more minds you explore, the more ideas you will uncover.

In my day-to-day operations mining has become a way of life. I think it is the only way for a top-level executive to function. The more pipelines you open, the broader your base of communications will be. I know that personally I bypass no chance to expand my "diggings." I am always on the lookout for opportunity leads. I pose an open question to any and all acquaintances: "What information can you give me that I can turn to profit advantage for my company?"

There is nothing unique about this philosophy of business life. Those of us who are full fledged members of the "Miners Guild" live by a kind of unwritten agreement. You tell me, and I'll tell you. On the one hand, we are all chronic foragers for profit information. On the other hand, we try to give back as good as we receive.

A typical case in point occurred about six months ago. I struck up a friendship with a banker at a cocktail party in New York City. Shortly after, the man visited Pittsburgh. A week or so later I received a call from him from the West Coast. He had just heard what he judged to be a unique opportunity relating to the textile machinery business. Knowing that this was one of our particular areas of interest, he thought it might be useful for me to know about it. I thanked him for the tip and had one of my key exploitation people follow it up. Within hours we consummated a deal with a foreign company that earned several thousand dollars for one of our divisions.

That's just the first half of the story. I owed my banker friend a favor. The opportunity to pay the debt arose recently when I heard about an underwriting proposition that seemed a natural for his company. I telephoned his office and learned he was in Rio on vacation. When I reached him in Rio, his reaction to my information was a sigh.

"You sound disappointed," I commented. "Doesn't the deal sound right for you?"

"It sounds too good," he replied. "For this one I'm sure I'll have to get back home in person. Which will not make me too popular with my wife."

This is just part of the dues you sometimes have to pay when you are a member of the Guild.

In any case, I hope the point I've tried to make is clear. The dynamic corporate miner is an aggressively gregarious individual. He is anything but a loner. And he chooses his moments to be quietly contemplative when he is not surrounded by people. To be blunt, he is an inveterate city hopper, table hopper, and party hopper. He is amiable and warm. His badge is a genuine smile of welcome. He circulates. He does not inhabit corners.

Do I find it a strain to maintain this pace? The question was posed to me recently, and frankly I had never thought about it before. I might find it a strain, I replied at the time, if I didn't enjoy it so darned much. It's true, you have to have a sincere liking for people to play the genial host as if you mean it. But I find this is no problem for most chief officers who, for the main part, have been carried to the top largely on their egoes. Only a small minority of the presidents I have met are genuinely shy and withdrawn.

I for one consider myself fortunate that I have not been cursed with this handicap. I thoroughly enjoy cultivating people at all levels. At stockholder meetings I make it a special point to circulate all over the place. I go out of my way to meet as many customers, employees, suppliers, members of the community, and outright strangers as I can.

I can recall one deal in particular that happened five or six years ago. As a result a small unprofitable enterprise of ours was spun off at a handsome gain, and a valuable new facility was traded in exchange. It was the perfect deal. Our loss became another company's gain, and we were able to milk a profit from an operation the other company had all but given up on. But the whole point of the story is this: the entire deal came about as the result of a conversation between a total stranger and myself while on a plane enroute between Milwaukee and San Francisco. Which only goes to prove—the more pipelines you put out, the more messages you will receive.

DON'T WAIT FOR THINGS TO HAPPEN; MAKE YOUR BREAKS

The poet Milton said, "They also serve who only stand and wait."

It's fairly obvious to me that Mr. Milton was no businessman. Experience proves that the businessman who spends too much of his time waiting will get left at the post. You get no prizes standing on the sidelines.

I can cite a dozen or more examples to support this premise. One company I can call to mind has a growth rate that is perhaps a third or less of its potential. About 15 months ago a meeting of the company's top brass took place over a three-day weekend. During these sessions some serious soul searching was done and far-reaching decisions were made. The main area of discussion concerned future plans and strategies of growth. Internal expansion, it was generally agreed, would take too long.

In recent years the industry had become increasingly dynamic. The company was being outpaced by leading competitors who were acquiring young technically oriented firms staffed by talented scientists with new vision and ideas.

The most important agreement reached was that henceforth a major goal of the company would be acquisition. And from that point on the chief executive seriously has thought of himself as an acquisition-minded president. He honestly intended following through with his company's projected course of action as set forth at that fateful meeting.

But intentions are sometimes easier to express than enforce. The president is an arch-conservative by nature. His background is mainly financial. He has conscientiously made a comprehensive study of what it takes to consummate a merger and make it work. He can cite chapter and verse of key factors that go together to produce the desired synergistic effect. And I suspect that he knows of a few factors the rest of us have not encountered as yet.

This is all to the good, I suppose. After all, the merger game is an involved and intricate pastime. You cannot over-learn the field. On the other hand, a president must be realistic. This man is not. He keeps hunting for that risk-free acquisition which we who have often traveled the merger route are convinced is little more than a wild and wishful fantasy. And while he waits for "ideal fits" and super-synergistic opportunities, his company's chief competitors are busy as elves consummating imperfect but relatively successful deals.

In 15 months our ultra-cautious president, who serves only the competition with his waiting philosophy, has completed just one successful acquisition. In line with stated plans and policy he should have made four or five. Understandably his board and his stockholders are growing increasingly impatient. I would not care to hazard a guess about what the future might bring. Perhaps the chief executive will continue waiting for that "perfect merger" to come along, although I have long ago concluded that this deal resides almost exclusively in the euphoric dreams of anesthetized presidents.

For his sake I hope he will soon get off the bench and into the game. Because, though he may be inclined to wait for his dream to come true, his board is more likely to have other ideas.

Smooth opportunity ruts

How many Profit Deactivators are at work insidiously under-mining opportunities in your company? If your operation is typi-cal, chances are that you play unwitting host to a horde of these gremlins.

A management consultant told me recently, "Every company I have ever come across has certain gray areas of profit motiva-tion where the president is resolutely pushing his people in one direction, and they are just as determinedly taking two steps backward for each step they've pushed forward. The reason is usually simple, and in most cases it centers around the buck. The trick in charting a profit course for the top and middle man-ager, I have learned, is to make darned sure that the course you chart for him is not in conflict with the personal profit course he may have set for himself."

A good example of this was alluded to in a recent issue of *Business Week*. The company under discussion was Fairchild Camera and Instrument Company. "When (Charles) Sporck was general manager of the semiconductor division," the article pointed out, "he decentralized the manufacturing function. Long an admirer of Alfred Sloan's management techniques at General Motors, Sporck gave each manager of Fairchild's six semicon-ductor plants wide authority to decide which products he would make. Since each manager was evaluated on the basis of the profitability of his plant, the managers chose the products that were easiest to make—those already in production with high yields. Only reluctantly would the managers start new products."

The profit exploitation need was apparent. But the proper in-centive was missing.

Profit Deactivators are touched off in another way, too, trig-gered in this case by decision paralysis generated from the top. The way it works is deadly, and it is more common than most presidents would like to admit. A small beauty products company serves as a perfect illustration of decision paralysis in action—or rather, inaction.

In this company which I fear is destined to remain small and unimpressive, three or four new products are introduced each year. Much rides on the success of these items. If two of them survive, the product development effort is considered profitable. If one survives, the result is close to break-down. If not one gains market acceptance, it constitutes a serious financial setback for the stockholders of the company.

The organization is strongly dominated by its chairman and chief executive officer, an autocratic executive who owns 70 percent of the stock. Every major decision or judgment is subject to his final okay, and at times his verdicts can be scornful and withering. I have heard a description of one manager who "emerged bathed in perspiration" from a session with the boss.

In view of this the climate for the creative exploitation of new opportunities and profit ideas is pretty much what one would expect. Every managerial judgment is prefaced by the anxious speculation, "How will the boss respond?"

The company's top-level brass are extremely well compensated considering the size of the company and the scope of dollar responsibility. In spite of this, the rate of executive turnover is high. The most recent emigré was the vice president of research and development. He took a one-third cut in income to join a competitor, and his only regret is that he didn't make the move months before.

"Working with the boss was bad enough," he told me. "What was even worse was that I couldn't get a straight answer from any of my associates. We would develop a new product in the lab, for example, and for a time be enthusiastic about the result. But when we showed it to the manufacturing and marketing people, they would invariably cast a damper over it. They would express vague reservations about the moistness, color, or consistency of the mixture. Nothing specific. Just general criticism. It's not quite right, but we can't say why. It took me a while to appreciate that all they were doing was covering themselves in anticipation of the boss's possible disapproval."

The situation in this company went from bad to worse. Today, in spite of a full laboratory staff on the premises, much of the new product development is done outside the firm.

"It was becoming increasingly embarrassing for me to justify the payment of fat royalties for development work," the research chief told me. "This is one of the superficial reasons for my departure. But the underlying reason—I guess you could call it decision paralysis. The president of the company is operating a regime of fear. I'm beginning to wonder if he doesn't get his kicks that way."

Extreme though the case may be, the pattern is not uncommon where autocratic chief executives display no tolerance for the fallibilities of human judgment. The net result is stalled actions and delayed decisions. The status quo becomes a safe harbor, and in such a port the ships of opportunity invariably sink.

Sidestep secondary problems

I have found that one of the toughest tasks facing a chief executive is the setting of proper time priorities.

I heard, for example, of a consumer products company's president who, in exasperation, issued what he referred to as the 1969 Ultimatum. The document was dated January 1st. It was prepared as much for the president's benefit as for his key people. Primarily the Ultimatum was little more than a list of activities the president intended to cut down sharply in the coming year. Included were such items as:

- Speeches before universities and associations.
- Personal visits to plants and other company facilities.
- Attendance at meetings of operating groups within the company.
- Reading of statements and reports.
- Participation in the financial operations of the company.

The Ultimatum made more than one person in the company unhappy. Executives from all quarters vie for the president's time. And every manager has his own strong convictions regarding what he feels to be urgent matters which warrant the chief executive's attention.

But in the end it is the president himself, sitting objectively at a wide-ranging vantage point, who must decide which matters are primary and which are secondary as far as the most profitable use of his time is concerned. And inevitably there will be other men who, evaluating presidential priorities from a more limited perspective, will be disappointed by some of his choices. To the PR man, for example, speaking before a group of influential investment bankers may hold the highest precedence. To the vice president of manufacturing, it may be of the utmost importance for the boss to pay a personal visit to Plant A so that he can have a firsthand understanding of the problems they are trying to cope with there. And who could argue the importance of any corporation's financial activities?

I am sure the president referred to above had all of these considerations in mind when he prepared his Ultimatum. But he had other things in mind too. I am assuming that he also reasoned that the items cited on his list were more delegatable than the presidential exploitation of opportunities relating to the development of new products and markets and the acquisition of new companies and facilities. Again it boils down to the old question: *What could I and should I be doing that I am not doing to the extent I would like to do it?* I think it is a good idea for a chief executive and for all executives to ask this question periodically.

My guess is that the president above, having posed this question to himself, replied that he should be devoting more time and effort to innovation and acquisition. He must also have concluded that the only way he could make more time available for such activities would be to cut down on what he ultimately judged to be secondary problems.

POLISH UP YOUR CRYSTAL BALL

I know a president whose company is known mainly as a textbook publisher. The president's son, Jim Jr., is a sophomore in college majoring in economics. One day he was given the assignment of preparing a case study on a company of his choice. Deciding to explore his own "back yard," he approached his father with pencil and pad in hand.

Jim Jr. reeled off a long list of questions. To several of them his dad replied, "You'll get a better answer to that one from Bill Jergens." Jergens is general manager in charge of the textbook division.

After the sixth or seventh buck-passing, Jim Jr. scratched his head, "You know, dad," he said bluntly, "for the head of a textbook publishing house, you don't seem too up to date on some of the things that are going on in the textbook publishing business."

His father smiled. "True, but why don't you try me on teaching machines, educational games, home computers, management training programs, or sales training records?"

Young Jim frowned. "What has that to do—"

"—with the publishing business? Everything," Jim Sr. said, and proceeded to instruct his son on the facts of presidential life.

You can probably work out the rest of the story for yourself. The textbook business, as the president explained, was of secondary interest to him. This aspect of the enterprise was steady, stable, routine. It was a known factor and in extremely capable hands.

"My stress as chief executive," he pointed out, "is on the profit opportunities of five, ten and fifteen years from now. That's why, though I may be stale on the bread-and-butter business, I like to think I'm right up to the minute in those other areas I mentioned."

This president's experience and philosophy lines up with my own. In my opinion the president, more than any other officer of the company, must constantly sight into the future. The Miner's Hat, don't forget, has a headlight on it. It was by following its beam that we got into the boat business. Exploring previously unconsidered opportunities, we found that the burgeoning yacht business had special appeal. We produce airplanes and a variety of products for automobiles and other vehicles. Why not boats? I asked my marketing and acquisition people to study the field. We liked what we learned and made arrangements to toss our hat in the ring through acquisition of Hatteras Yacht Company of High Point, North Carolina, the first company in its field to market luxury cruisers with fiber glass hulls. This was just the start. The crystal ball is still in full use. We are currently also in houseboats, for one, with the purchase of Whittaker Marine and Manufacturing, Inc.

The trick, of course, is to project into the future. Another industry which must inevitably mushroom involves the manufacture of textiles and textile machinery. We know that in the underdeveloped nations, for example, people will not be content for long to gird themselves in fig leaves and sandals. Thus North American Rockwell has become especially interested in this field. Our Draper Division, I have mentioned, is the world's largest producer of automatic looms. And our TMW Knitting Machine Division is one of the nation's leading producers of knitting machines for a variety of products.

How does the manufacture of boats and textile machinery tie into our more basic business of auto and truck components, aircraft, missiles, and electronic gear? The same way teaching machines, educational games, and home computers tie into the publishing business. The answer is profit opportunity. You un-cover it wherever and whenever it is to be found. Mainly, as I have said, it is a matter of gazing into the crystal ball and reading the signs. And essentially, the task is the president's.

What kind of signs am I talking about? Take manufacturing methods as an example. The signs here tell us that traditional methods will be increasingly challenged and changed by techno-logical developments and ideas. The company that pioneers such change will obviously be a giant step ahead of the competition. And it is the chief executive's responsibility to see to it that his company is a leader and not a follower.

Here, as a case in point, is the idea of controlling a knitting machine electronically. The idea is not new. But its technical development has long eluded the efforts of textile researchers. The situation is fraught with opportunity. Intending to cash in on it first, we have combined the advanced electronics capabilities of our Autonetics Division with the practical experience of our tex-tile engineers. The result, hopefully, will be the electronic auto-mation of knitting machines. Another important profit goal we are shooting for is the electrostic spinning of yarn. The process under development, Electrospin, is jointly owned by North American Rockwell and Scientific Advances, Inc., a subsidiary of Battelle Memorial Institute.

I hope you get the point. The message I am trying to put across is the same one the president I just talked about tried to hammer home to his son. A tomorrow-minded president has neither the time nor the inclination to be bothered with the day-to-day activities of the business. Naturally he keeps his finger on the overall pulse of the operation. He checks profit performance and keeps tabs on the achievement of goals. But the only time he worries about the routine aspects of the business is when it is called to his attention through a tripping of controls that things are not going right. His main overriding concern and obligation relates, not to the problems of today, but to the opportunities of tomorrow.

GIVE YOUR DREAMERS TIME TO DREAM

In January 1967, Frederick G. Donner, then chairman of Gen-eral Motors, told the Economics Club of Detroit, "We in this country have a built-in confidence in our ability to expand, to discover and improve all things. We live in a society where the light is always green for go. Innovation has been—and is—our way of life."

I couldn't agree more. But I must also point out that in no organization will innovation just happen. You have to *make* it happen through the excitation of ideas by trained and talented people. Important as the Miner's Hat may be for the top executive —and I've said earlier that I systematically put aside time for my own reflection—it should be stressed that his company's mining activities should by no means be confined to his own endeavors.

One executive who agrees is Commander Edward Whitehead, chairman of Schweppes U.S.A., Ltd. He states the case as follows in *Dun's Review:* "Creative management demands that the chief executive of the company be receptive to new ideas and new approaches to old problems. The president must ask himself constantly: 'Is the climate of this organization such that new ideas will germinate and flourish?' 'Do I encourage exp imentation?'"

I would add a further question to this list: "Do I give my dreamers time to dream?"

The other day one of our people who handles manufacturing services approached Ed Williams, the Commercial Products Group's sharp, tough-minded vice president of manufacturing. As Williams describes it, he had that "certain glow" in his eye. What this man wanted was to take a survey of all the round, flat, and square steel used in our various plants throughout the nation. His objective was to find out what sizes were used, and in what quantities.

Williams asked why he wanted the information. Well, he said reflectively, he had been mulling over an idea relating to the procurement of steel that could save three million dollars a year if the volume checked out as expected. He had been attending seminars, he said, studying write-ups and talking with technical people. He showed Williams a breakdown of what he had come up with and his boss was interested indeed.

Whether the idea worked out or not is beside the point. Here is a profit opportunity of the first magnitude. In some companies, ideas of this kind are expressed freely and abundantly. In other companies they are difficult to come by, and then only from a handful of men on the very top rungs.

What determines the difference?

In my experience it is time. Key managers in dynamic companies are busy people. But we do our best at North American Rockwell to see that they are never too busy to sit back from time to time to think and dream. I don't care what job an executive holds, whether he is responsible for purchasing, finance, or personnel. I assume that one of his primary duties is to exercise his imagination on behalf of his company.

I strongly believe that each manager should build into his daily schedule a cushion of time during which he can lean back at his leisure and ponder everything in general and nothing in particular, giving his mind full rein to take off in any direction it pleases. Because, as has been pointed out by more than one sage observer of the business scene, it is all very well to talk about group effort and teamwork, and brainstorming quite definitely has its place. But when you boil it down, most of the truly outstanding ideas that have helped to make our country great have been conceived by solitary men with time on their hands, their eyes fixed contemplatively on the walls in front of them.

GET THROUGH TO YOUR PEOPLE

I know a president who, taking salary, bonus, and options into consideration, earns about $350,000 a year. This amounts to approximately $7,000 a week, or $175 per hour. They are figures that the chief executive likes to get across to his people.

"No asset of the company is worth more than the president's time," he has been heard to remark. "If people understand the value they will learn to treat his time with care and consideration."

He may have a point. But in my view his attitude produces more harm than good.

I have seen his key executives in session with him. The atmosphere is charged with tension. Visits are precisely timed to the minute, and by the 14th minute of a 15-minute session, the boss's barely perceptible glance at his watch becomes more eloquent than a shouted dismissal might be.

The benefits of the approach are obvious. The president plans his time with super-efficiency. He permits nothing to divert him from his pre-set schedule.

But in my view he pays dearly for his lack of flexibility. Most of the damage is subtle and psychological. I have heard complaints from key associates that confirm my personal feeling.

"He's a minute-hand fanatic," one executive informed me. "What's worse is that most of the time you're with him you spend listening. He issues instructions, and you take notes. When he's done he asks if the instructions are clear. If you say yes, he is pleased. If you need additional explanations or information his annoyance shows through. And even if he brusquely complies, there is rarely enough time left to do the job right. All in all, communicating with him is a harrowing experience."

I think a president owes it to himself and to his people to get across his ideas with unmistakable clarity. "Too busy" never was nor will be a valid excuse for muddled communications. If a chief executive can spend 15 minutes to dispatch a lieutenant on an opportunity trackdown, he can spend 15 minutes more if need be to make sure the subordinate does not set off for a tin mine to prospect for gold.

For my part I would be mildly suspicious of a president who is consistently vague in making his desires understood, or who makes himself unaccessible to his people when they need further enlightenment. I would wonder how he ever got to be president without communicating effectively. Or if he were being intentionally vague in order to shift responsibility for a particular action or decision to a subordinate.

A New York management consultant recently told a group of manufacturing executives: "The chief executive with a hard-to-access ear forces a difficult mental conflict on his subordinates. Consciously or not, they form a value judgment in their minds: 'What will stand me in worse stead with the boss? Going back to him for the information I need? Or muddling through the best way I can with my limited understanding?' Too often, unfortunately, the latter route is selected, and the ultimate result is to water down the profit opportunity that is involved."

I too recognize that few assets are of greater value to a company than the hours and minutes of its top executive team. On the other hand, if a particular project or area of exploration is worth my time at all, it is worth as much of my time as is required to get maximum yield out of the vein that's being mined.

CHAPTER TWELVE

The Hat of the Super-Salesman

Nowadays, of course, the super-salesman in industry wears a trim, stylish hat of the very latest model. Nevertheless, I have chosen the bold bowler of the old-line drummer as my Hat of the Super-Salesman. Foolish and out of style as he is, the drummer or trunk peddler had something to teach modern businessmen, including presidents. His wisdom was that he knew his job was *to sell,* and he made no excuses for it.

Does it offend your sensibilities for me to say that a good chief executive has to be, among his other accomplishments, a good salesman? I hope not. He had better be a *super*-salesman or all those other accomplishments of his stand an excellent chance of going to waste.

Salesmanship, of course, is held in low repute in parts of the intellectual community and even in parts of the business community, which should know better. *Fortune* can proclaim that selling is "the cutting edge of a free competitive economy," but a great many businessmen aren't convinced. The entire marketing function is still often regarded as no more than a necessary evil, and as for personal salesmanship in a chief executive—well, that's just not mentioned in polite society.

But I believe these critics object more to the word than the function. A "salesman" still conjures up an unfavorable image in many minds. The boss doesn't want to be a "salesman," perhaps, but he doesn't mind being a "persuader," especially a "great persuader." Call it what you will, the president of a company must be highly skilled at the persuasive arts. He must be a convincer of great ability. He must be—let's face it—a super-salesman, because he is the one who is finally responsible for:

—presenting the company's case to the public;
—dealing with stockholders and the financial community;
—persuading employees to get behind important programs;
—representing the company *vis-à-vis* government;
—serving as the company's number one personal salesman.

The fact is that in a democracy, persuasion is all-important. You just can't get anything done without it. And any large organization such as a corporation must have a measure of democracy in both its internal and its external operations. This factor has been getting a great deal of stress in modern management concepts, with the result that today's new breed of corporation president is more a great persuader than ever. It's no accident that many progressive corporation presidents have gone into another type of persuasion—politics—with success.

Senator Charles Percy of Illinois, to take one good example, has so far been able to sell his policies and himself to both local and national audiences. A glance at his background is most instructive.

During his sophomore year at college he organized something called the University of Chicago Cooperative Fraternity Purchasing Association. What he did was call door to door along fraternity row, and talk to purchasing stewards about saving money by co-op buying of foods and services. For instance, he reduced laundry prices from 7½ to 3½ cents a pound by channeling all the business to one laundry.

Chancellor Robert M. Hutchins called him "the richest kid ever to work his way through college."

Percy was elected president of Bell & Howell at the age of 29, and he was a super-selling president of the first order. Among his many selling feats, he sold the New York Society of Security Analysts on letting him use a film with his presentation (at the time, audio-visuals were against the Society's rules), and he sold Bell & Howell employees on a retirement plan that was tied to company profits ("In a capitalistic society," he told employees in speech after speech, "it's best to *be* a capitalist.")

Finally, as an "old" man in his mid-30's, Percy got into politics. He went to Washington to talk to the House Ways and Means Committee about a low-tariff policy. He was supposed to testify for 20 minutes but more than two hours later he was still talking —and almost hypnotizing the protectionist Congressmen with the power of his persuasion.

"If I had your salesmanship and flow of language," complained Daniel A. Reed of New York, "I might be able to do a much better job of defending my position."

What is this quality of almost matinee-idol forcefulness, possessed by a politician like Percy or John Lindsay of New York? It's the same quality possessed by every great actor or great politician. I call it "profit histrionics."

THE POWER OF "PROFIT HISTRIONICS"

Let me tell you what happened to me not long ago. This inventor wanted to tell me about his product—something I was reasonably certain we would have no use for. But I agreed to a 30-minute appointment because you can't afford to pass up any new product opportunity, even when the chances of usefulness are remote.

Unlike some inventors, this young man turned out to have a rare gift of self-expression. He began talking and in a few minutes I was all but enchanted. He got my attention, led me into what he was saying, and aroused my curiosity until I was as interested in his invention as he was.

I cancelled my next appointment, then another one after that. I spent two hours with him, and after he left I asked myself, "Was I intrigued with the invention or the man?" And I knew it was the man. He had been literally on fire with his idea, hammering across impressions so strongly that I couldn't help but listen. I was sold on the man because he had been an effective *actor*. Now I had to take a long, hard, cold look at the product itself. There were, in fact, possibilities, and we later came to terms with this inventor to our mutual profit.

The question is: would I have studied the product as carefully if the man hadn't been so forceful a salesman? I like to think I would—but I'm not sure. Fortunately I'll never have to answer the question because that inventor was a master of *profit histrionics*.

Any successful chief executive must have the same technique. He must have that magic gift of getting other people interested in the things *he* is interested in. He must be able to generate enthusiasm and get people to respond to what he is saying, so that later on, when they analyze it, the logic will come through to them.

The president must be, in short, a bit of a performer. Among other things, this means that he should *enjoy* the spotlight. The enjoyment might be a very quiet thing that no one would ever notice or suspect, but it must be there all the same.

"A salesman must get the recognition factor; he must be able to share the thrill of a sale and solving a customer's problem," as the marketing vice president of Citgo was saying the other day. It's as important to him as salary. The same thing applies to a "super-salesman"—the president. There is a rich profit pay-off for the chief executive who, in his own quiet way, can manage to be something of a ham.

"Profit histrionics" isn't just performing, of course. It implies superb organization of your thoughts, and astute use of facts and figures. I recall hearing about a lady sales manager for a small Atlanta frozen foods company. They had a new way to freeze seafood—a real breakthrough in cryogenics that resulted in an incomparably superior product. But it wasn't enough to just show the product and have it admired. Big sales aren't made that way.

Before approaching one national restaurant chain, this young lady visited dozens of their places, checking the seafood quality and price. She made educated guesses about their costs in various parts of the country, and when she finally made her first call on national headquarters she had an amazingly accurate set of "guesstimates," comparing costs of existing products vs. the new one.

She had a better mousetrap—but it had to be sold. And she got a fabulous long-term order after only two calls. It was her well-documented "profit histrionics" that did it.

This concept applies to all kinds of situations involving persuasion, and in this chapter I want to discuss many of them in some detail. First, however, let's make a check on your own powers of persuasion. Let's take the following test: The answers are not Bible, of course, but they should start you thinking.

TEST YOURSELF: ARE YOU PERSUASIVE?

Situation number one

You're giving a talk at a professional seminar. You've labored long and lovingly over your presentation which involves complex visuals and makes what you consider a vital point about current industrial methods. You've gone to the trouble to rehearse, and your presentation times out exactly to the 50 minutes you have been allotted. But now, on the day of the seminar, the schedule is chaos. Several speakers have droned on past their time and now you're on. You look at your watch and realize with horror that it's only 20 minutes until lunch time. Already the audience is restive, bored. All right, do you . . .

   a) Rush through the presentation, cutting as you go, and get them out on time or close to it?
   b) Wade through every last word and every last slide, figuring that after all, they paid to hear this and they might as well get it all?
   c) Start in as dynamic fashion as you can, and in 15 minutes take a vote on whether the audience wants to hear a brief summary or the rest of the speech?

Situation number two

A government agency has indicated that they are about to rule favorably to your company in a very important case. But the final notification is delayed. Day after day goes by and you're getting anxious. Your information is that it's all settled, but you can't help but wonder if something has happened to upset the decision. What's your move?

   a) Just sweat it out, at least for a couple of weeks more.
   b) Figure out some excuse to write the agency and ask for clarification on some technical point of the expected ruling.
   c) Get your eyes and ears in Washington to work and tell them to find out exactly what's going on.

Situation number three

Your "devil's advocate" on the New Products Committee is overdoing it in this month's meeting. He's shooting down every suggestion with ill-tempered questions about costs and marketing procedures that really can't be answered yet. His questions will have to be answered eventually, of course, but meanwhile he's blackballing some highly promising ideas. As the presiding officer, you think over what you should do and finally decide to . . .

a) Gently but firmly shut him up at least for today; one more negative remark from him is going to drive you out of your skull.
b) Have notes taken on each of his objections and give instructions that answers are to be given at the proper time —but not now while general concepts are being discussed.
c) Let the men making the proposals field the questions; it's good for them.

Situation number four

You've just concluded an acquisition that is going to synergize your company like nothing you've ever pulled off before. For a time it looked as if the owner of the smaller company, a wry, humorous little man, was going to sell to someone else, but today in a personal meeting he has accepted your offer. As you prepare to take your leave, you . . .

a) Congratulate him again on his decision, and wind up the session as quickly as you can.
b) Just to make sure he doesn't change his mind, re-state your argument once more, shake hands and leave.
c) Kid around with the old boy about the mistake he almost made when he was thinking about selling to the other outfit.

Situation number five

You've got the answer to a cost-control problem that had been haunting the company the last three quarters. This is going to mean a great deal in terms of profits and you can hardly wait for the board meeting to start so you can unfold your revelation. It crosses your mind, however, that the board has been giving you a little static lately, and your plan does involve a moderate investment in equipment. What's your strategy at the meeting?

a) Leap right in with the good news, trusting that you can sweep aside any dissent with the enthusiasm you truly have for the plan.

b) Start out by painting the grim picture of the problem as it has existed for all these months. Mention actual, painful cost figures. Then catch them by surprise with your unexpected solution.

c) Let the meeting develop as it may, and then when you judge it's the exact correct psychological moment, throw in your cost-control solution almost casually, letting it slowly sink into their heads.

Situation number six

Your wife wants you to take a winter vacation this year but you're not at all persuaded that you should try to get away from the office at this particular time. So you handle your wife this way:

a) Tell her you'd probably have to rush back for a few days, to take care of the problems that can be expected to arise, and the trip would be ruined if you tried to go now.

b) Listen to all her arguments, and weigh them before responding.

c) Sell her—hard—on the super-special summer vacation you promise to take if she'll just forget about the winter trip.

COMPARE YOUR ANSWERS WITH THESE

Situation number one

We started with an easy one. My correct answer is (*c*), which gives me a chance to hold the audience if I can, and gives me an out if I can't.

Situation number two

Chances are good that many of you picked (*c*) here, and it's true that you should have some agents finding out what they can about the situation. However, my best answer is (*b*), for a reason having to do with the psychology of persuasion. In many experiments, psychologists have shown that your chances of getting agreement are better if you can get the subject to *commit himself* in writing. In other words, it's difficult for him to change his mind

once he's gone on record. In this letter to Washington you're trying to get some statement indicating that things will go your way.
It's a delicate operation, but if you can bring it off you'll sew up
the ruling.

Situation number three

Here there is room for argument. There is some justification for
all three answers, but I would select (c). Your "devil's advocate,"
after all, is on the committee to be just that. And it will do the
proposers good to have to come up with answers to difficult questions. Will the situation kill off any creativity? It had better not—
and that's where *your* persuasiveness comes in.

Situation number four

Call in one of the company's top outside salesmen and ask him
what he would do. Very probably he'll go for (a), and so would
I. Any salesman knows that when you get the order, you get out
as quickly as possible. The man's mind is made up. Why hang
around and ask for trouble?

Situation number five

Here opinion might be divided between (a) and (b). The
argument for (b) runs on the psychological principle that a solution is more effective when you first "arouse desire" on the part of
the audience. However, presumably your board is well aware
of this problem and needs no more than a brief review. I would
choose (a) and I would sell my solution just like that inventor
who called on me about the new product.

Situation number six

Without trying to advise you on your personal life, I would
suggest (b). This is what is known as a "dialogue," and I think
you can trust yourself to open one with your wife. Let her persuade you if she can. Are you so sure you can't get away now, if it
means so much to her? As for (a) and (c), she's heard all that
jazz before.

If you got as many as five "right," you are a persuasive fellow,
at least in my book. At any rate, you and I see eye to eye on
selling strategy. Without taking the results too seriously, the test

should give you an idea of how well you do in what might be called "textbook persuasion." Let's briefly review some of the principles involved.

THE ELEMENTS OF PERSUASION

First of all, let me state as clearly as I can that persuasion, or salesmanship or whatever you want to call it, is not a logical thing. It is basically irrational because it appeals to the emotions and to certain habits of thought that seem to be common throughout humanity. Your argument itself should be logical and should be capable of point-by-point analysis. But it won't get that analysis unless it is presented in such a way that people will listen. And this presentation, this salesmanship, is not really rational.

However, here are some guidelines:

1. Get their attention

The beautiful logic of your sales pitch means nothing unless they're listening. It's as simple as that. If you believe in what you're saying, your evident sincerity may do the trick. If your personality is dynamic, forceful—or if you look the part of a smart, hard-driving chief executive—that might do it. There are times, however, when you have to resort to a little gimmickry. The communications consultant Michael St. John once began a film about a new product with the titles, a mighty roll of symphonic music, and a promising flash of color—followed by the words "The End." The idea was to jolt the audience into attention. Don't hesitate to try some tricks of your own like this.

2. Try early and often for a commitment

If you can't "close the sale," work for agreement on various points that get the prospect in the habit of agreeing with you. I've already discussed this, and every salesman knows that it works. Get some kind of commitment in writing, if possible, and try to have a third party present so that the commitment will be a matter of public record. This is a powerful push toward persuasion, and one of the best ways to get it is to consult in advance with your target audience. In other words, a cost-cutting program works best if the people who will carry it out have had a hand in developing the plan. It becomes their "baby," and they'll fight for it.

3. Know the emotional content of your argument—and use it

If you're offering recognition, financial rewards, or some other basic value, make sure your audience knows about it. A basic point, but one that's often overlooked. Don't be so subtle, so sophisticated that you leave out the "gut issues."

4. Recognize group pressures

Some people are more subject to social pressures than others, and different people respond to different kinds of pressures. For example, a scientist who regularly tells the vice president of research to keep the heck out of his lab might be thoroughly intimidated at any hint that his peers in the world of science think he is on the wrong track. Again, a martinet type is usually best persuaded through an appeal to higher authority. In any case, though, the man who doesn't respond to some group pressure probably has yet to be born.

5. Ask for a lot

Various psychological studies show that the more "opinion change" you ask for, the more you are likely to get. Ever notice that the President always asks Congress for more budget than he expects to get? The reason is that if he asked only for what he thought he would eventually get, he would actually get far less.

6. Remember that the first element of persuasion is trust in the persuader

If your audience trusts you they will probably trust what you are saying. Relate, then, to each individual as a person. Find some common ground of agreement that will inspire him to believe that you and he think alike. But never let him forget that in this situation *you* are the expert, a person whose advice he can take without fear.

Those are some of the things that make some people persuasive. Often a president (or a salesman or anyone else) uses these elements without actually understanding them. Then we say that he is "naturally persuasive." But it is perfectly possible to train yourself to be, in fact, a super-salesman.

Now let's relate; let's tie it together. Let's apply what we know about persuasion to some of the situations when a president must be his company's first and best salesman. If you recall, we mentioned these situations at the beginning of the chapter. Some of them are, far from incidentally, the same situations when a president must also be his company's star reporter. Now let's take them one at a time.

TARGET NO. 1—THE PUBLIC

In its massive, well-planned campaign to counteract the unfavorable publicity it had been getting, Dow Chemical Corporation appointed one man as its spokesman in all matters pertaining to student action against Dow recruiters on campus. This one man was to assess each situation as it came up and give the company position to all news media. Any guess who it was?

If you said the head of the company, you're right. Herbert D. Doan, president and chief executive officer, was the one man to be called on all questions of company policy in this context.

Of course the public relations department planned the program which included visits to "hot" campuses in advance of the Dow recruiter's calls, special training for PR men who would appear on the scene, the dissemination of press information, and a system to insure that the company's side of any controversy would get into print and on the air. But Doan instructed the PR staff to keep him informed almost minute by minute of any riots or student boycotts, and all statements were issued in his name and with the full weight of his office.

The Dow position, as articulated by Doan, seemed reasonable to most observers. Of 618 editorials in localities where there had been anti-Dow demonstrations, only 11 took a stand against the company. Consumer sales apparently were not suffering, although Dow didn't try to minimize the damage the student action might have done to its "image."

Here was a situation in which the president took personal charge of a sensitive, complex, and dangerous public relations problem. He made sure that his staff provided him with all the updated information that could be assembled, then he went before the public as the company's one spokesman. It was courageous, and it was also effective.

And let me say that now, at this moment in history, every company president has a great responsibility to be a super-salesman of free enterprise when he talks with the young. I'm not arguing the merits of Dow's manufacture of napalm, one way or the other. I'm simply saying that the president must be a salesman not just for his company but also for our system and our way of life. Let's stop compromising our convictions.

TARGET NO. 2—STOCKHOLDERS AND THE FINANCIAL COMMUNITY

Now here is a job for a super-salesman, and no mistake about it. How do you tell the annual meeting that although profits didn't go up as much as you planned this fiscal year, things are going to be better next year? How do you justify expenditures to one of those professional shareholder representatives who delight in tweaking the chairman's nose? And here's a problem that comes up more and more: How do you justify your company's investment in the community through the training of minority group members, aid to urban renewal, the arts, etc.? There's no way to prove that these things contribute to profits. Can you persuade your shareholders that there is such a thing as corporate citizenship? If you're a salesman, you can.

Turning to the question of dealing with security analysts, I've noted that the fear of making improper disclosures has caused many chief executives to stop talking to analysts. Or when they do give presentations, they load them down with too many films, slides, samples, and other "fluff," withholding hard facts. I believe that this is largely a mistake.

"People in the analysts meetings are human beings and they can be motivated by the same sales techniques as TV viewers," a New York public relations man once told the *Wall Street Journal*. This is, of course, nonsense. Analysts are not casual consumers but tough, hard-nosed investigators. Some of them are considering boycotting presentations of companies that substitute fluff for facts.

It's part of the president's job to see that no one gets special or inside information that is not available to all. But any public company should keep in more or less constant touch with interested analysts. And no good salesman ever tried to work without facts.

I remember one company whose stock took a sudden leap upward just after it had made its semi-annual presentation to the New York Security Analysts. Was the president happy? He was livid. He called in the assistant treasurer, who had been charged with financial community relations, and raised the devil.

"The fact that our stock jumped after the presentation shows that you have *not* been communicating with the analysts," he said. "Why in the world should it surprise these fellows that our sales projections and earnings forecasts are great? They should have known, and our stock should have been making a gradual, steady gain for months."

It is, ultimately, the president's job to see that favorable communications are maintained with both stockholders and the financial community. You must assign the responsibility for day-to-day operations and see that it's carried out, and you must also take the lead in arranging special events such as field trips. Long Island Lighting Company is one utility that has on occasion flown analysts on helicopter tours of its marketing territory. And recently Kennecott Copper Corporation took 54 security analysts for a 48-hour sightseeing trip to its Utah mines, mills, and research center. Commented one analyst: "Pictures in an annual report can't begin to tell the story."

A word about your formal presentations: the analysts want earnings and sales forecasts, information about research and development, capital spending—the hard facts and projections. Skip the company's recent history; they already know that. One company spent three months and $20,000 on a movie to tell analysts its history and management philosophy, and, I would judge, wasted every penny of it. Skip the jokes, too; the analysts have probably already heard them. If you're in doubt about how to handle the meeting or what to say, attend several of the luncheon meetings at which companies in your industry give the presentation. See what the competition is doing—and how it's received.

One last thought: above all, what the analysts try to assess is the quality of your company's management—meaning you. They want to look at the man at the helm and see what kind of guy he is—and what kind of men he is training to back him up. Can there be any doubt that the chief executive must be his company's chief salesman?

TARGET NO. 3—YOUR EMPLOYEES

Here, more than in any other area, is a crying need for "profit histrionics." For example, what could possibly be more boring to

the average employee than dull old cost-cutting? It sounds negative, picayune, just plain tiresome. But it's vital if the company is
to move ahead. Your job is to sell your employees on it.

How? In this case, your greatest weapon is the truth. You must
go to your managers and spell out the areas they should be investigating. You must get them from your own past history, your
current records, and your knowledge of what your competitors
are doing.

Documentation is all-important. Don't just tell a manager to cut
costs, because that's not something he can pass along to his
people. Show him, make him believe that it is a thing that can
be done.

The first element of persuasion, remember, is trust in the persuader.

Take the area of procurement. At North American Rockwell we
emphasize what we call labor control. It has to do with productivity, with getting more goods out of a fixed investment. If I can
increase the number of axles that go through a process by eight or
ten percent, I have made a tremendous cost reduction per axle.
And it can be done.

So *persuade* the manager in charge by first convincing him that
you know the operation and that what you are telling him is true.
Use the elements of persuasion. Get a commitment from him, for
instance, by bringing him in on the planning. Recognize the emotional content: success in this project can mean advancement for
him. Don't hint at it; tell him. And ask for just a little more
improvement than you are secretly willing to settle for. Every
good administrator must know how to use the carrot and the stick
at the same time.

If you're on somebody's back once or twice every day, it begins
to wear off. What you have to do is establish a policy of *expecting*
top performance—imaginative, aggressive leadership from all departments. Then subordinates will begin to monitor their own
performance. But the philosophy, the whole atmosphere, must
come from you, as manifested by well-timed and well-structured
memos, conferences, etc.

The technique of persuasion is, as I was saying, irrational. But
the core of your argument must be logical. It must be truthful.
Otherwise, when your subject gets around to analyzing it, your
argument will fall of its own weight. And when it comes to fury,

a woman scorned can't hold a candle to a manager who thinks he's been sold a bill of goods by the home office.

Truth is the most powerful of all weapons. Consider, for example, the time we had to close a Wyoming plant that had become ours as part of an acquisition. Productivity was good; labor relations were better. But the plant was snowed in so much of the year that transportation was an insurmountable problem. Moreover, the plant duplicated another modern and excellent facility already in operation. Our studies showed that only one of the plants could be carried profitably and competitively.

Three months before the day we had chosen to shut the gates, we brought all the 100 employees together. Our vice president of manufacturing and facilities was there and he outlined the straight and simple facts, answering all questions as fully as he was able. Each of the employees actually seemed to understand our position. We appealed with them to stay with us to the end, to help us fulfill our obligations—and we offered a generous severance agreement to all employees who cooperated.

We half expected a rush for the exit. But very few of the employees left us. You get the best results when you level with people.

The mistake many presidents make in sensitive situations of all kinds is to bottle up communications until the last possible moment, hoping to keep the information secret. This, of course, is futile. The grapevine does its work and makes the problem sound worse than it actually is. Once again, it is the president who must "sell" the truth.

There was this one small metalworking company in the upper midwest. It had just been unionized, and it was having its first strike. What had happened was that many assembly crew members had failed to meet standards and had been dismissed en masse. The union reacted bluntly, but the president of this little company arrived to make a personal appeal. "Let me show you what I'm talking about," he pleaded.

He and six of his key executives rolled up their sleeves and put in a day's work on the assembly line. They showed that the standards they had set were not unreasonable. Then the president offered to reinstate the entire work force if they would agree to abide by the regulations. They did, and relations between the company and its union have been remarkably smooth ever since.

A salesman would say that the president put on a "darned good demo." I'd say he put on a good show of "profit histrionics."

Then there was the small tube mill in Wisconsin that had enjoyed an excellent thrift plan, keyed to stock performance, for some 20 years. One year, however, there was a market downturn and the fund's assets dropped. Employees were furious because nothing like that had ever happened. To compensate, the parent company put all hourly employees on salary and gave them the entire non-union benefit program. Yet the union won an election anyway, by three votes. The problem was later traced to autocratic and clumsy handling of employee relations by a local official. One man had ruined the company's otherwise carefully constructed plan. Don't let this happen to you.

TARGET NO. 4—GOVERNMENT

Most executives will tell you that there is no trickier form of industrial salesmanship than presenting your company's wants and needs to the massive complex of federal, state and local government. But I will tell you no such thing.

What is government? It is people. You don't deal with the FTC, FCC, FHA, IRS, or any of the other ingredients in the federal alphabet soup. At least, you shouldn't deal with them as such. Instead you should talk to the very human beings who are representing these agencies just as you are representing your company.

Experience has taught me to think of government liaison as a man-to-man, personal thing. Don't surround yourself with expensive legal insulation. I know of one food company that, when confronted with a labeling problem, swept down upon the poor defenseless little Department of Agriculture with about a half-million dollars' worth of attorneys, advisors, and consultants of all manner. They might have intended to intimidate somebody, but it didn't work. They had to change the label, when actually the rights of the situation were quite debatable. Another food company, in a similar situation, sent one modest company president to discuss the case with one government official, and the result was complete agreement.

When dealing with the government, don't get forbiddingly formal or legal. And don't try to go over the heads of the working stiffs who are assigned to deal with you. In the first place, lines of command in Washington aren't all that firm.

Think of the individual in government as a prospect like any other prospect. And think of yourself as a salesman like any other salesman—however super.

FINALLY, BE THE COMPANY'S NUMBER ONE SALESMAN IN ALL PARTICULARS

It's up to you. You are "Mr. ABC Manufacturing." Never forget it. You are never too busy to push the product a little.

There's such a thing as being too statesmanlike. When you were on that TV panel discussion the other night, for instance, did you manage to sit there with a profound smirk on your face for an hour and a half *without once mentioning the brand name?* If so, you should be ashamed of yourself.

Yes, we've all got something to sell, and if you are the head of a company, the person who is directly responsible for the livings of perhaps hundreds of breadwinners, then you'd better lower yourself down into the marketplace.

I'm not saying that you have to wear a product facsimile tieclip or drive a decaled company car. I am saying that you must remember that you *are* the company. You speak for it, dress for it, walk for it, eat for it, sleep for it, go to the theater for it.

Does that sound too crass, too commercial? Good. Then we're both talking about the same thing—super-salesmanship at the corporate level.

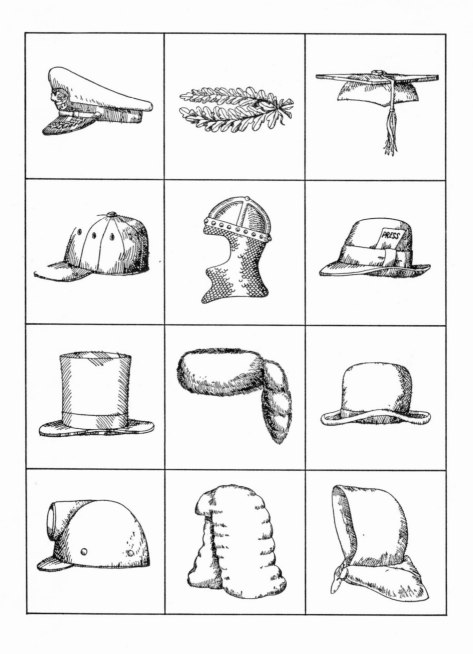

CONCLUSION

And now that you have perhaps a clearer idea of what it is like to be the head of a company, you just might be asking yourself: Is *anything* worth all that? But I hope you're not.

I've tried to make clear that to me there are unparalleled rewards just in the *doing* of business. And, of course, there are the financial and other physical benefits. It has been pointed out that few corporation presidents become extremely wealthy by today's standards, that their $200,000 or $300,000 a year, plus stock options, usually permit only the building of a relatively modest estate.

However, there is also a larger reward, relating to the idea of self-actualization which I discussed more than once in this book. To illustrate, let me call your attention to a report I came across the other day. It was issued by a group of social scientists at Harvard University.

We've all heard about the impersonality of technology and the crushing weight of corporate society, and how these forces are snuffing out individualism. We've heard it so often that some of us almost believe it. But this Harvard study of "Technology and Society" came up with quite a different conclusion. Studying our current period of turmoil, the scholars decided that people actually have *more* individualism, not less. Our system of wide personal and social mobility, our rich diversity of choice, and our broad range of experience make Americans "the most genuinely individualistic people in history." All this has led to a transitional period of strife, in which self-assurance causes people to make greater and greater demands—but with considerable luck and hard work we can reconcile the self-fulfillment goals of all, the report indicated hopefully.

It went on:

This is probably the first age in history in which such high proportions of people have felt like individuals. No 19th Century factory workers, so far as we know, had the sense of individual worth that underlies the demands on society of the average resident of the black urban ghetto today.

Despite the very real and very serious problems, then, it would appear that America has already succeeded in changing man's image of himself for the better. And the underlying force behind it all is the technology of the post-industrial age, as initiated and directed by business.

To help solve the problems, to help lead such a society, to help bring the world toward the kind of opportunities of the individual spirit that could be just around the corner—what higher calling in life could anyone have?

Index